COLORING FOR DANIEL

*An Adult Coloring Book for
Hope, Strength, and Healing*

*35 Positive, Uplifting
Coloring Pages by 32 Artists*

This book is dedicated to Daniel Savage and his family.

Credit for cover images:

Front cover image: Teresa Brown

Back cover images, from left to right, top to bottom:

Antonina Kalinina, Heidi Berthiaume, Cece Raven, Suzy Joyner, Kim Flodin, Olivia Julius Junggat, Cristin Frey, Sue Chastain (Colorist: Kelly Taylor), Shelah Dow, Annyce Turlea, Mary-Margaret Marx, Ligia Ortega

Book assembly by Cece Raven

With Assistance from Kim Flodin

This Book Belongs To page by Cristin Frey

Dedication written by Heather Johnsgaard

Cover design by Ligia Ortega

Coloring for Daniel
An Adult Coloring Book
for Hope, Strength and Healing

ISBN-13: 978-1539969686

ISBN-10: 1539969681

Daniel's book of Gnomes: An Adult Coloring Book
of Gnomes Throughout Time
is now available on Amazon.com
or visit his Facebook Page at
facebook.com/savagescribbles

The Dedication of Art

There is soul in art. Did you know that?

Through every pencil stroke, every paint splotch, or ink line, a person has put their soul into that piece. Whether it is the happy moments showing through, or the sad moments being remembered, it doesn't matter; as long as their creation sits in this world, their souls are with us..... forever!

Artists have a way, through their vision, of helping others see the world through different eyes.

It is with hearfelt emotions that we, a united group of artists, have come together to dedicate this book to the family of artist Daniel Savage, as they wade through the battles of the illness of Daniel.

As all artists do, we hope you find enjoyment in our art and want you to know that your purchase of this book has helped in the lives of one family.

Our thoughts and prayers are with the Savage family during this difficult time. May your beliefs be strong, your hearts healed, and may your life always include art.

All proceeds from the sale of this book are for the Savage family to help with their expenses. All images are copyright to the respective artists and does not transfer to the Savage family nor to any of the colorists.

Contributing Artists

Agy Wilson
Annyce Turlea
Antonina Kalinina
Cece Raven
Color Me Forum
Collette Fergus
Creative Life Studios
Cristin Frey
Genevieve Crabe
Hannah D'Agostino
Heather Johnsgaard
Heidi Berthiaume
Julie Thompson
Kim A. Flodin
Lianne Lynch
Ligia Ortega

Linda Franklin
Margaret Gates Root
Maria Wedel
Mary-Margaret Marx
Olivia Julius Dunggat
Pam Vale Branch
Paola Minekov
Samantha J. Decker
Sarah Clark
Shelah Dow
Steve Turner
Sue Chastain
Suzy Joyner
Teri Sherman
TigerLynx
Katie Savage

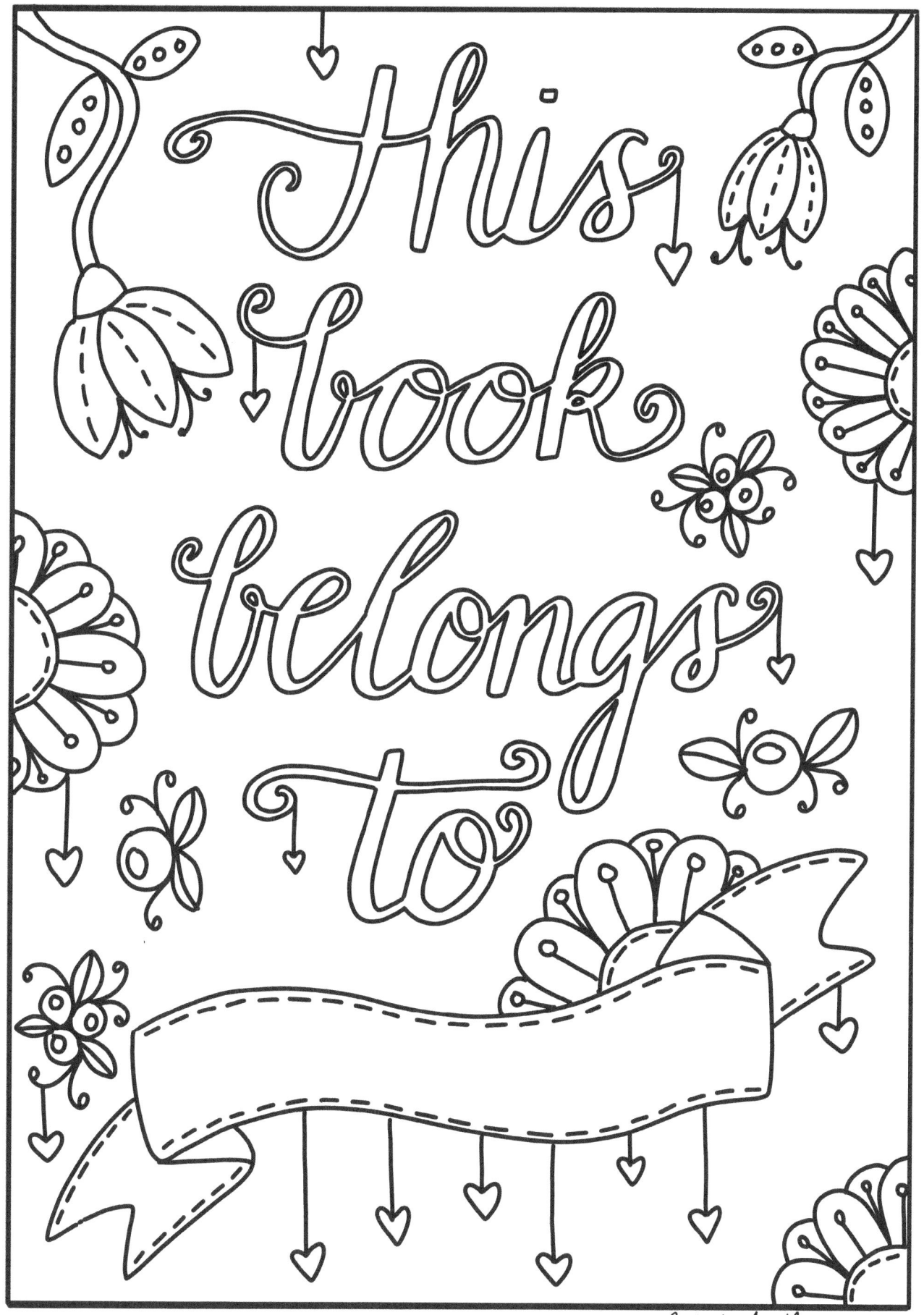

Goodbyes are for those who love with their eyes, because for those who love with their heart & soul there is no degree of separation.

-Rumi

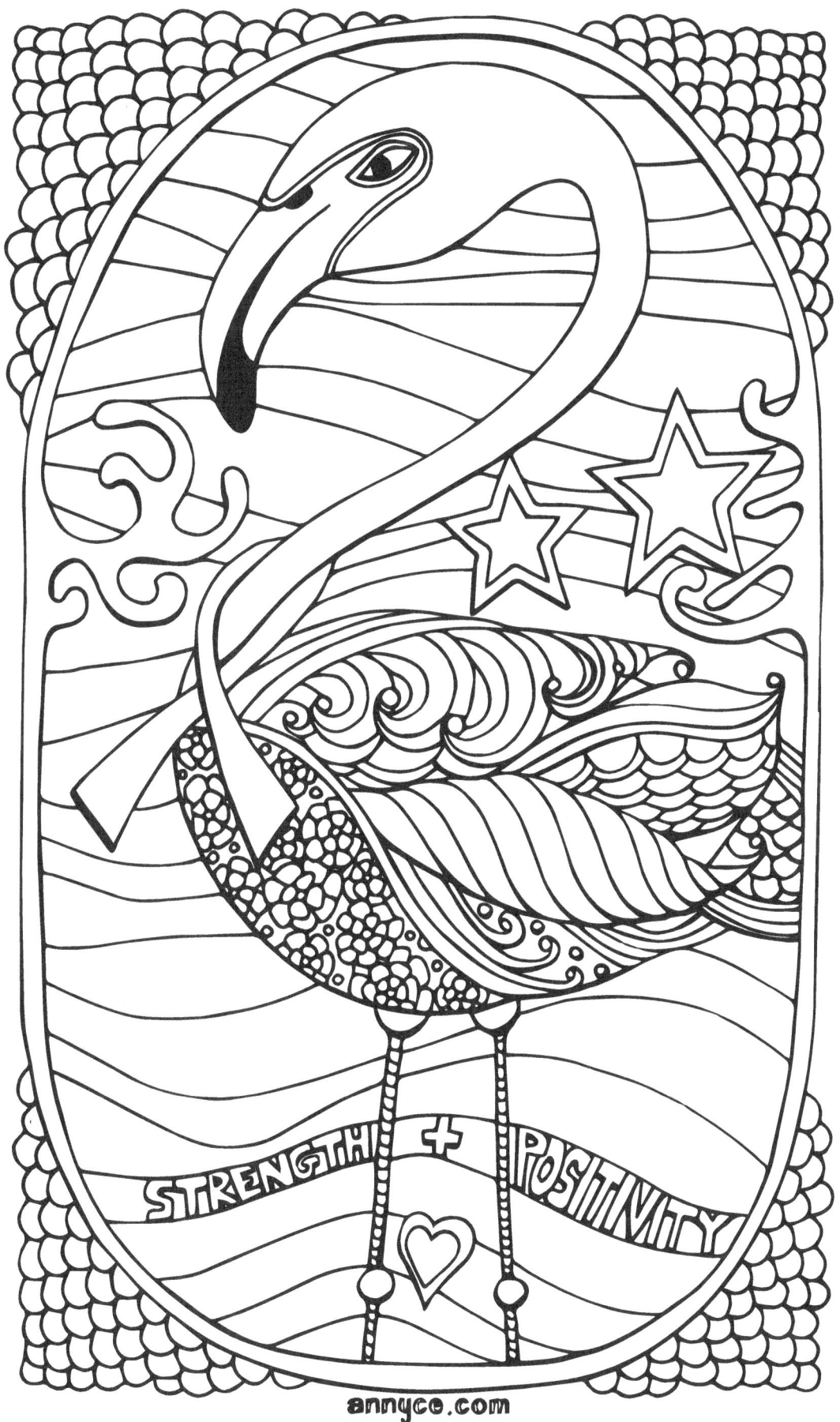

STRENGTH + POSITIVITY

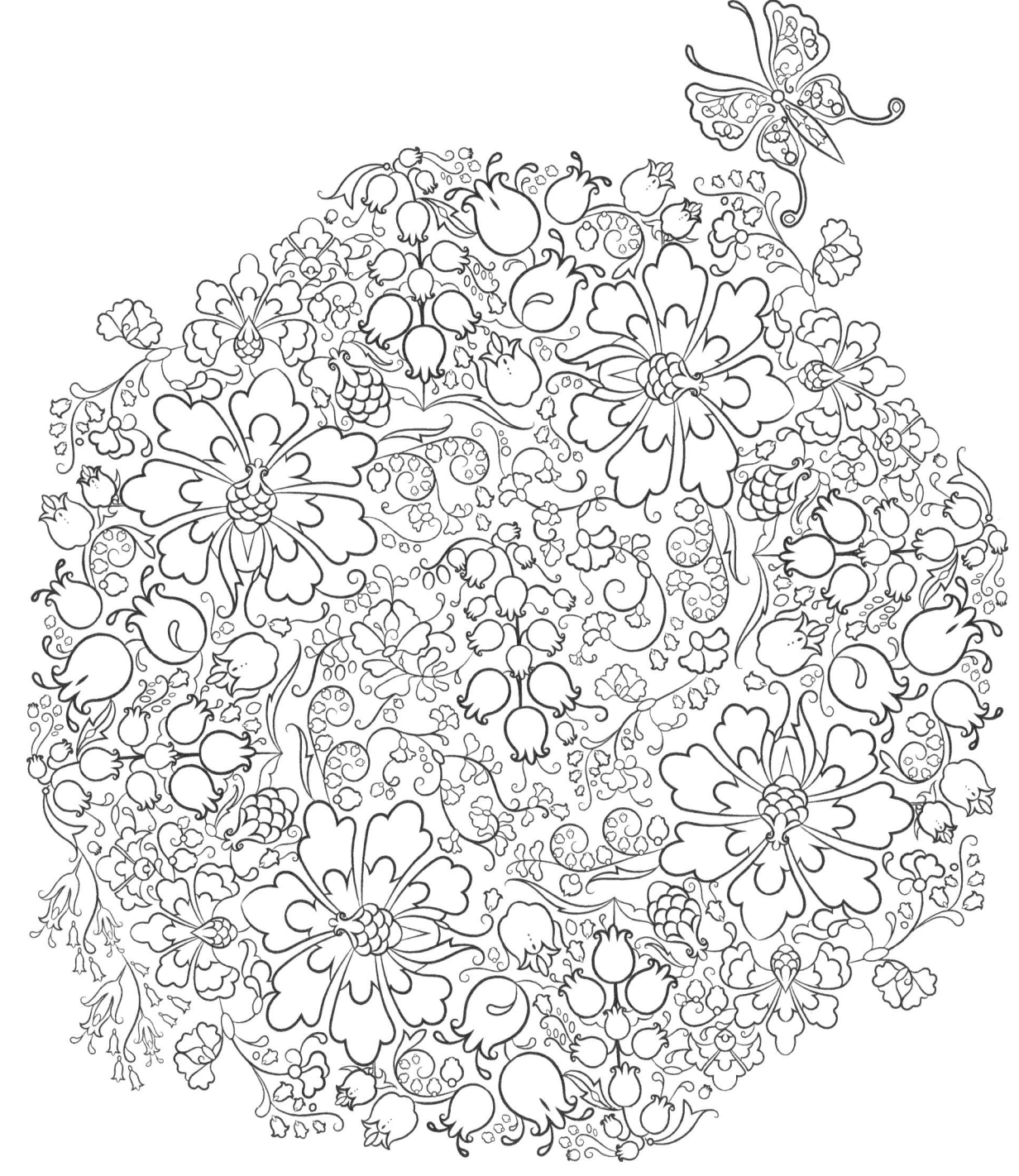

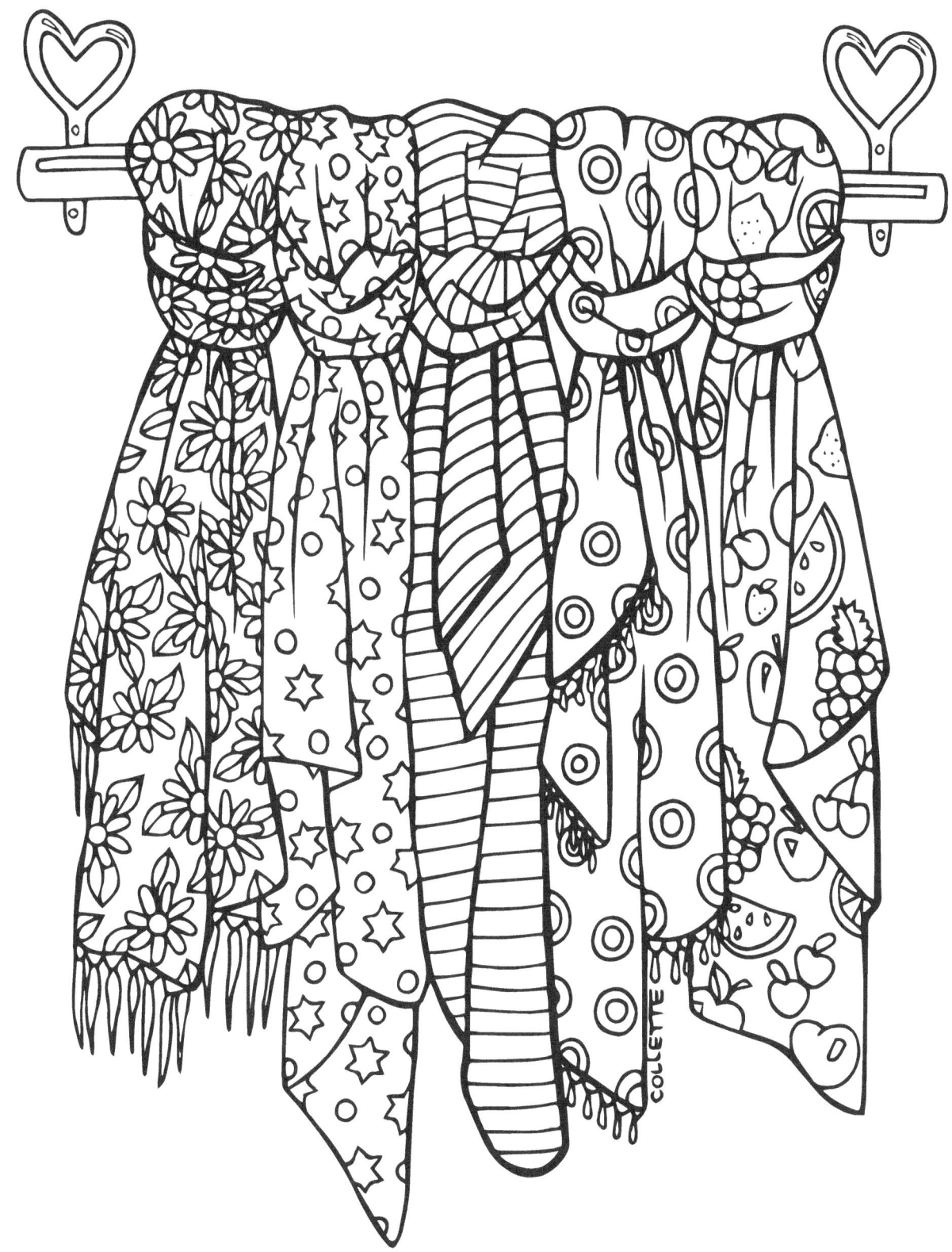

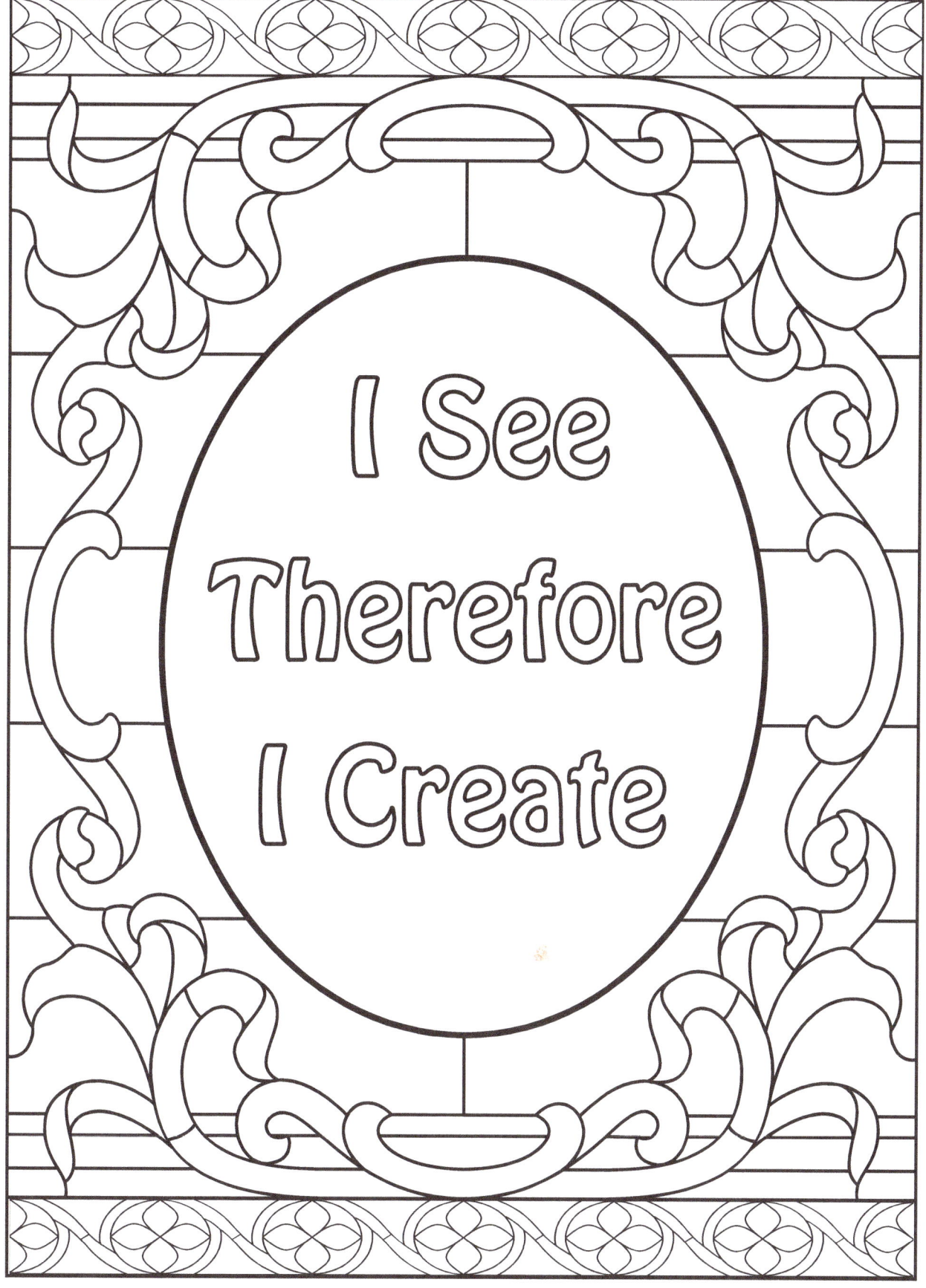

I See Therefore I Create

You can't live a positive life with a negative mind

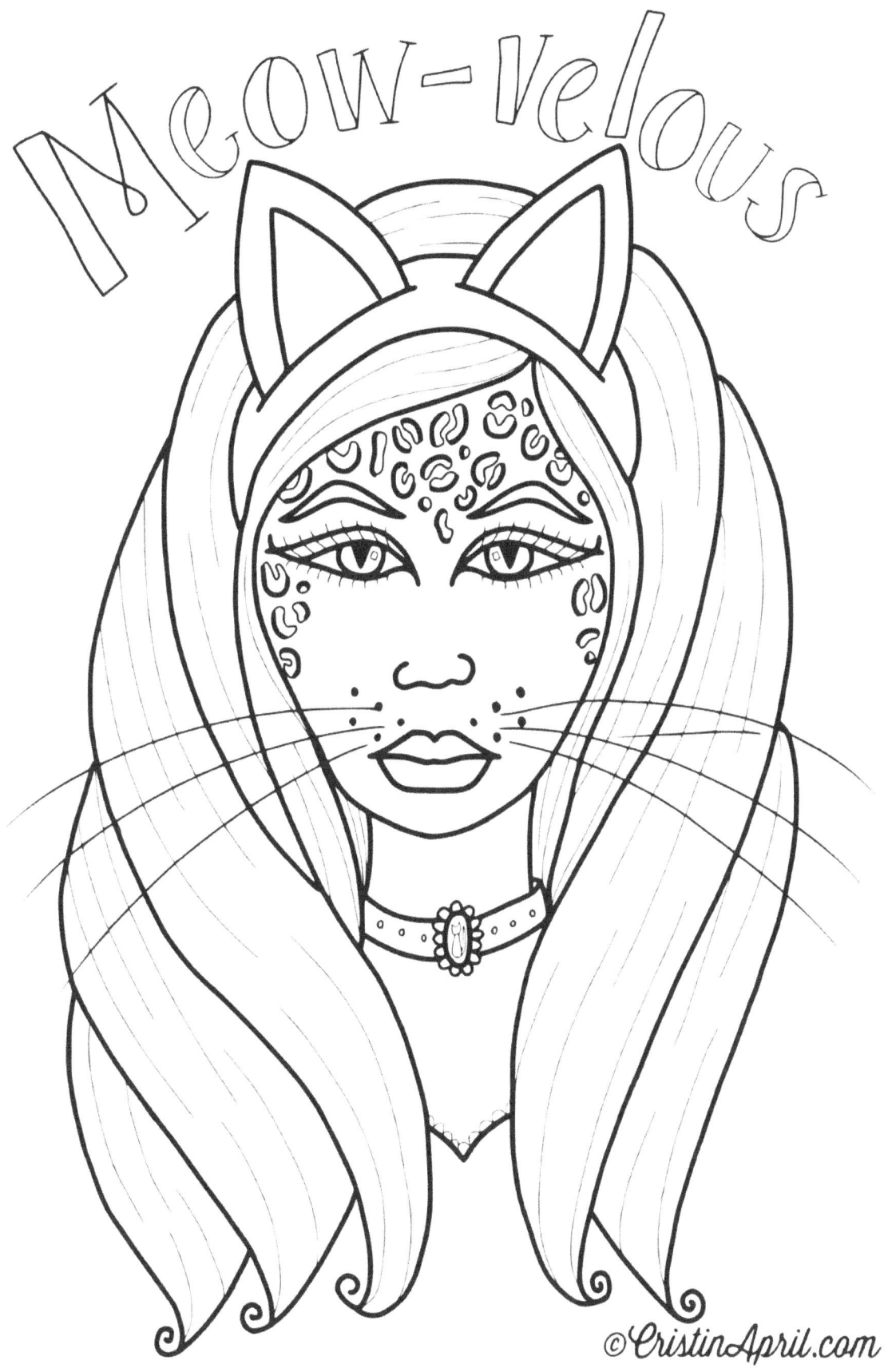

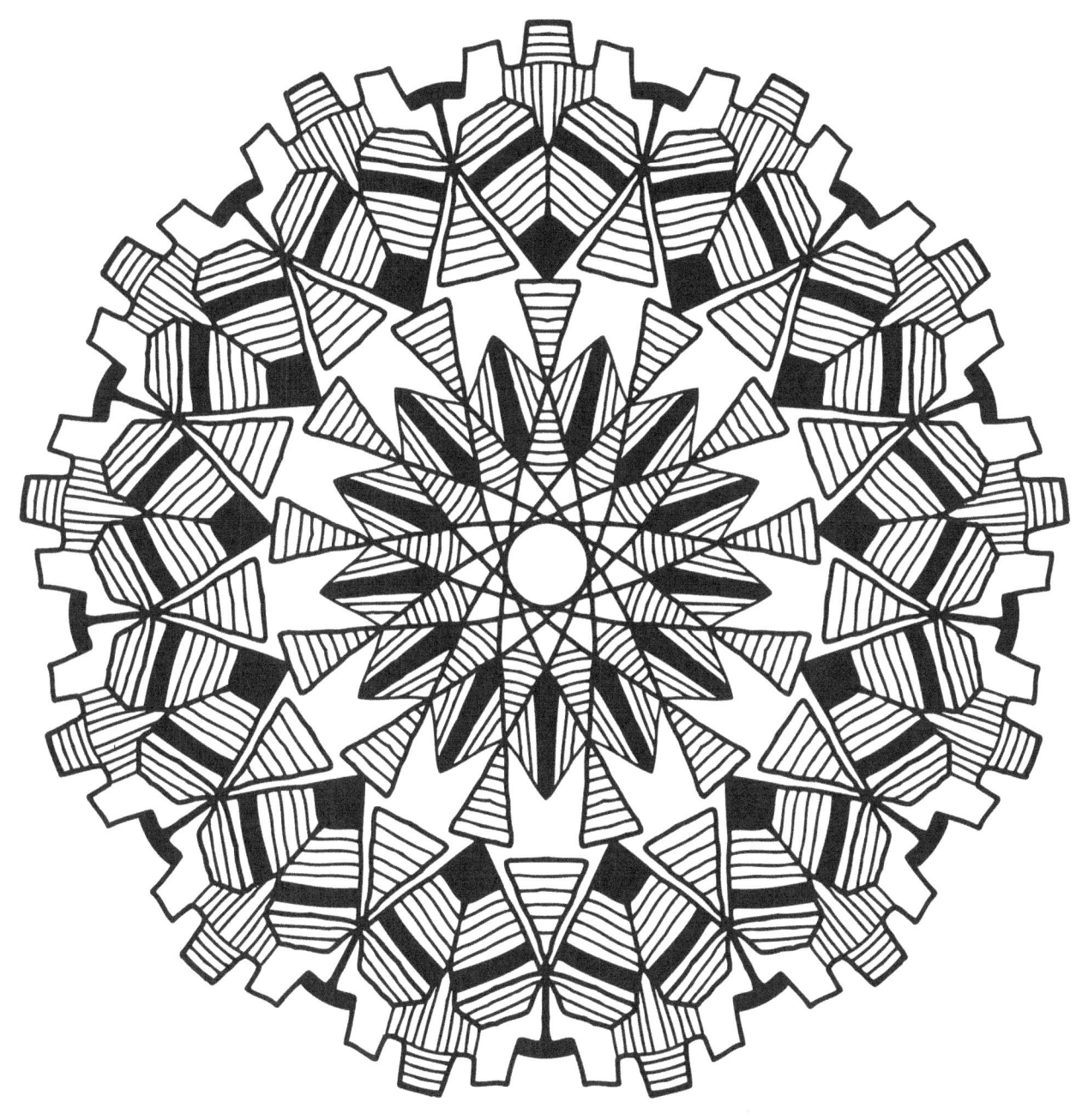

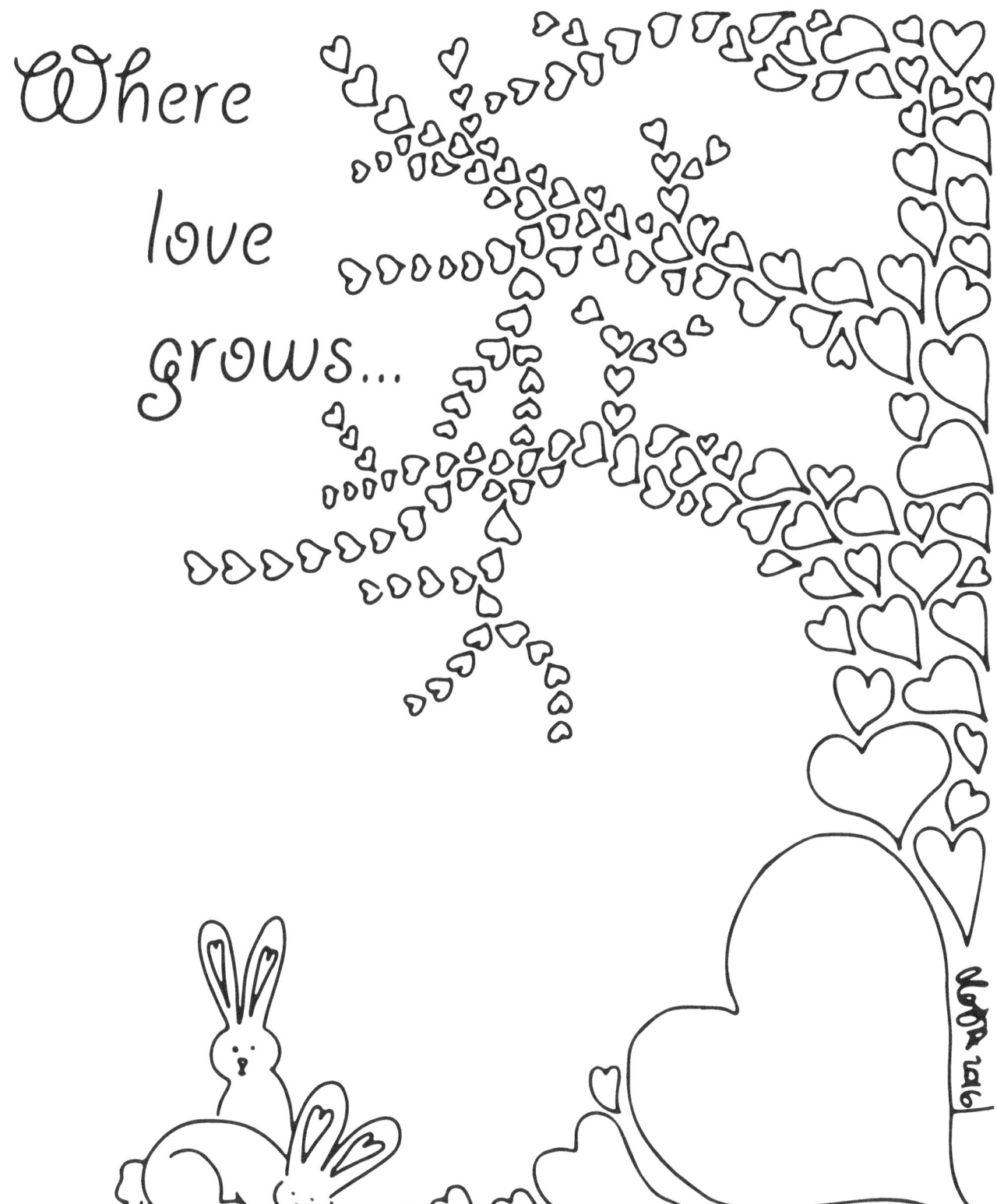

Where love grows...

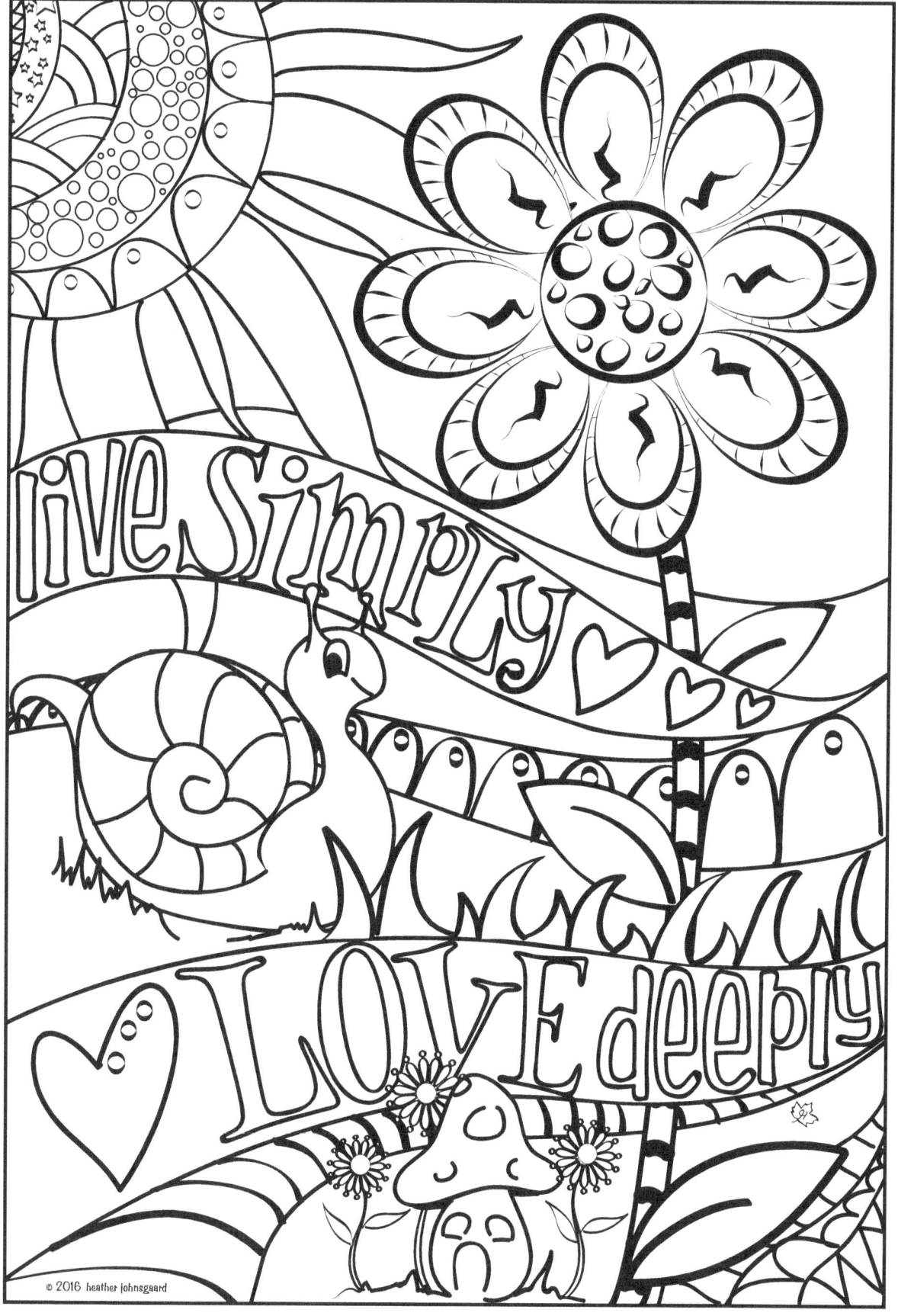

© 2016 heather johnsgaard

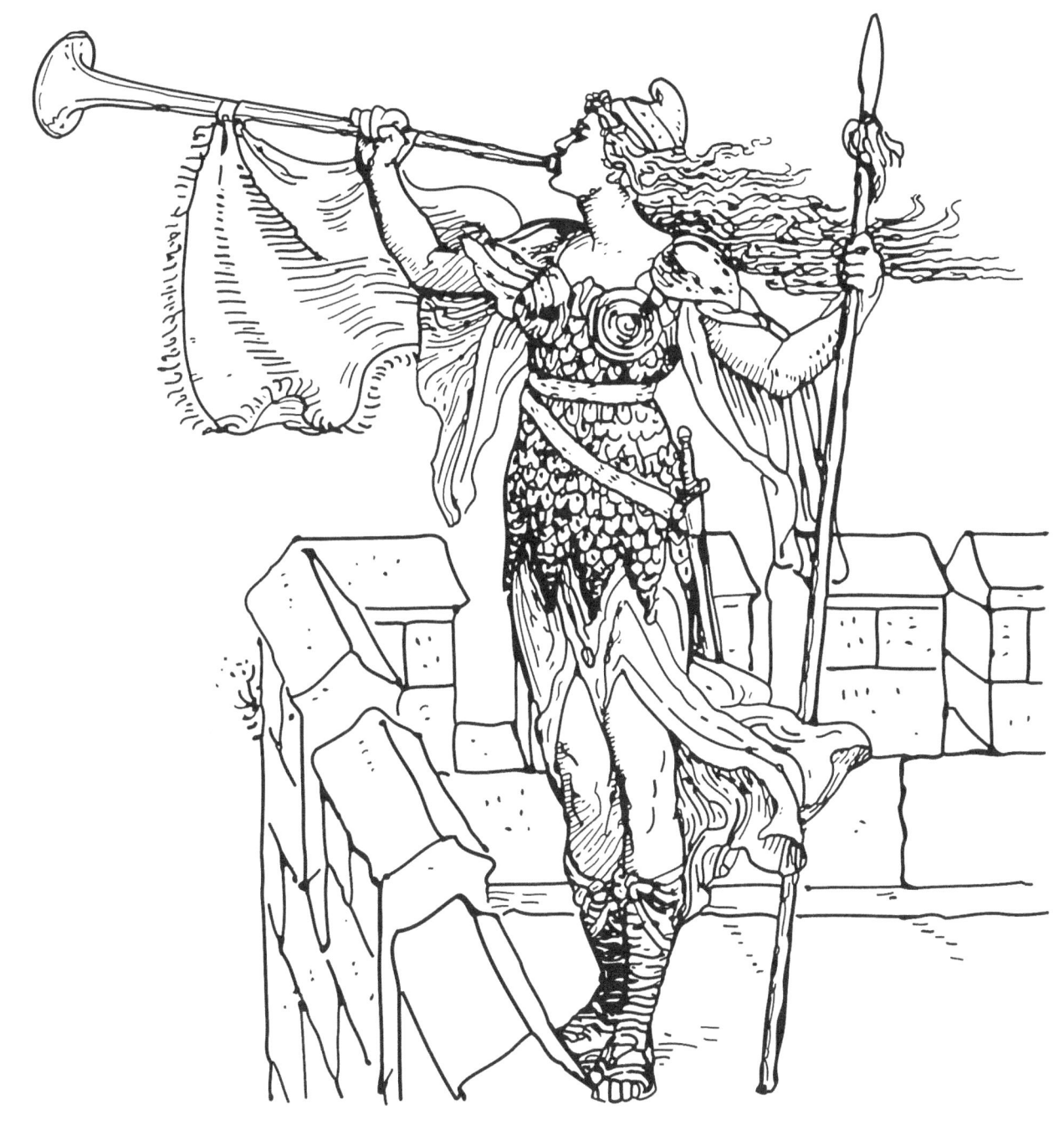

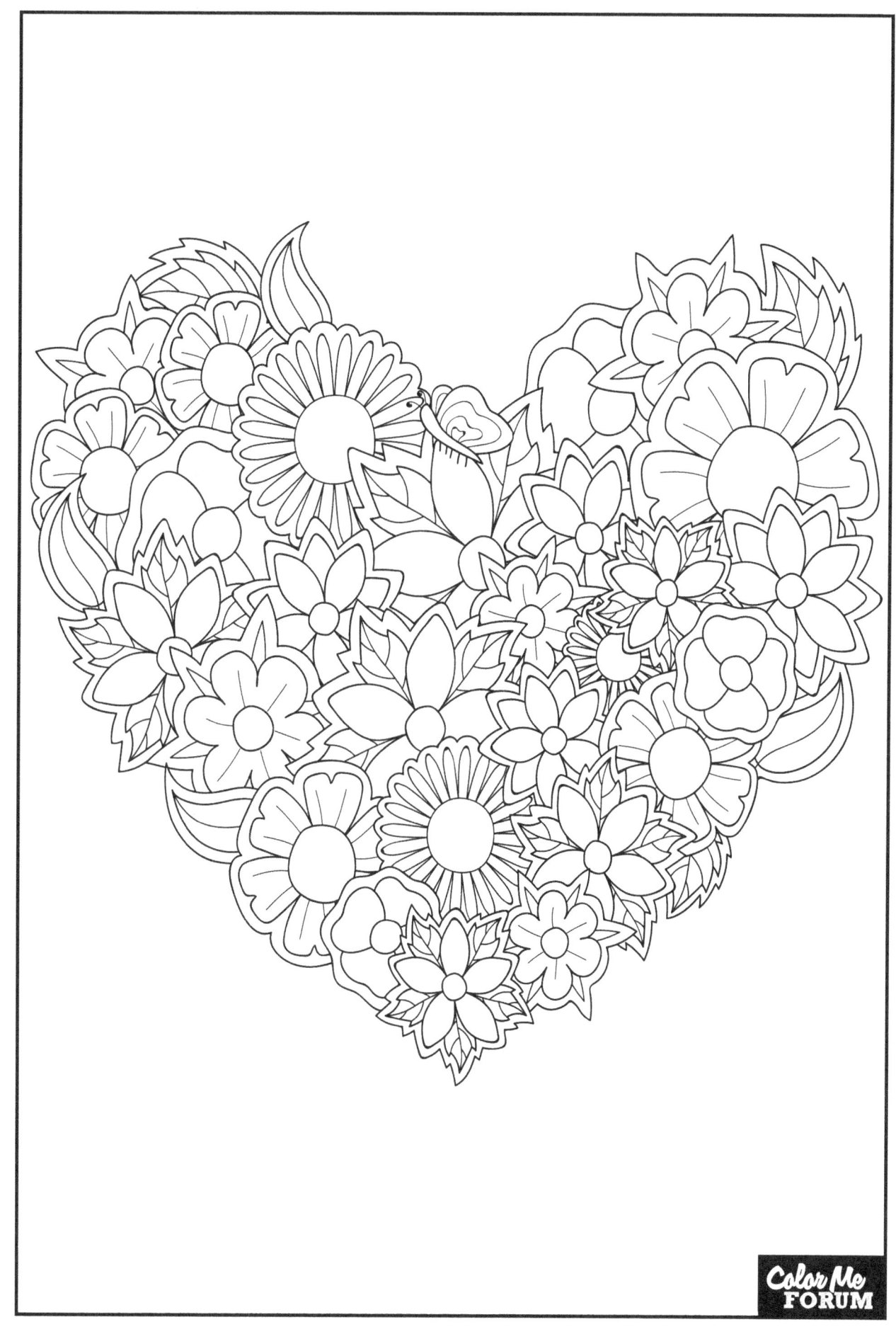

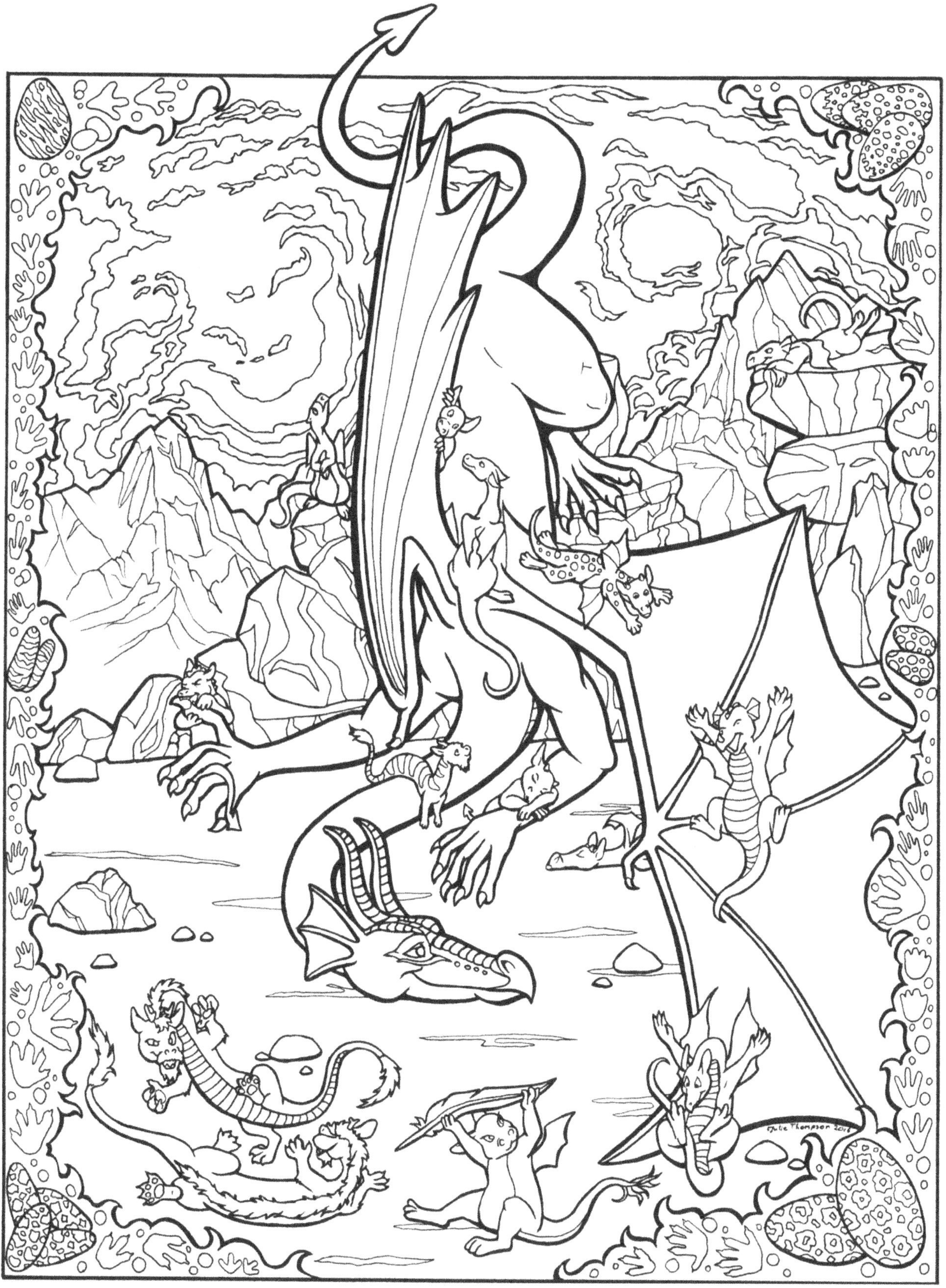

Julie Thompson www.featherlady.net

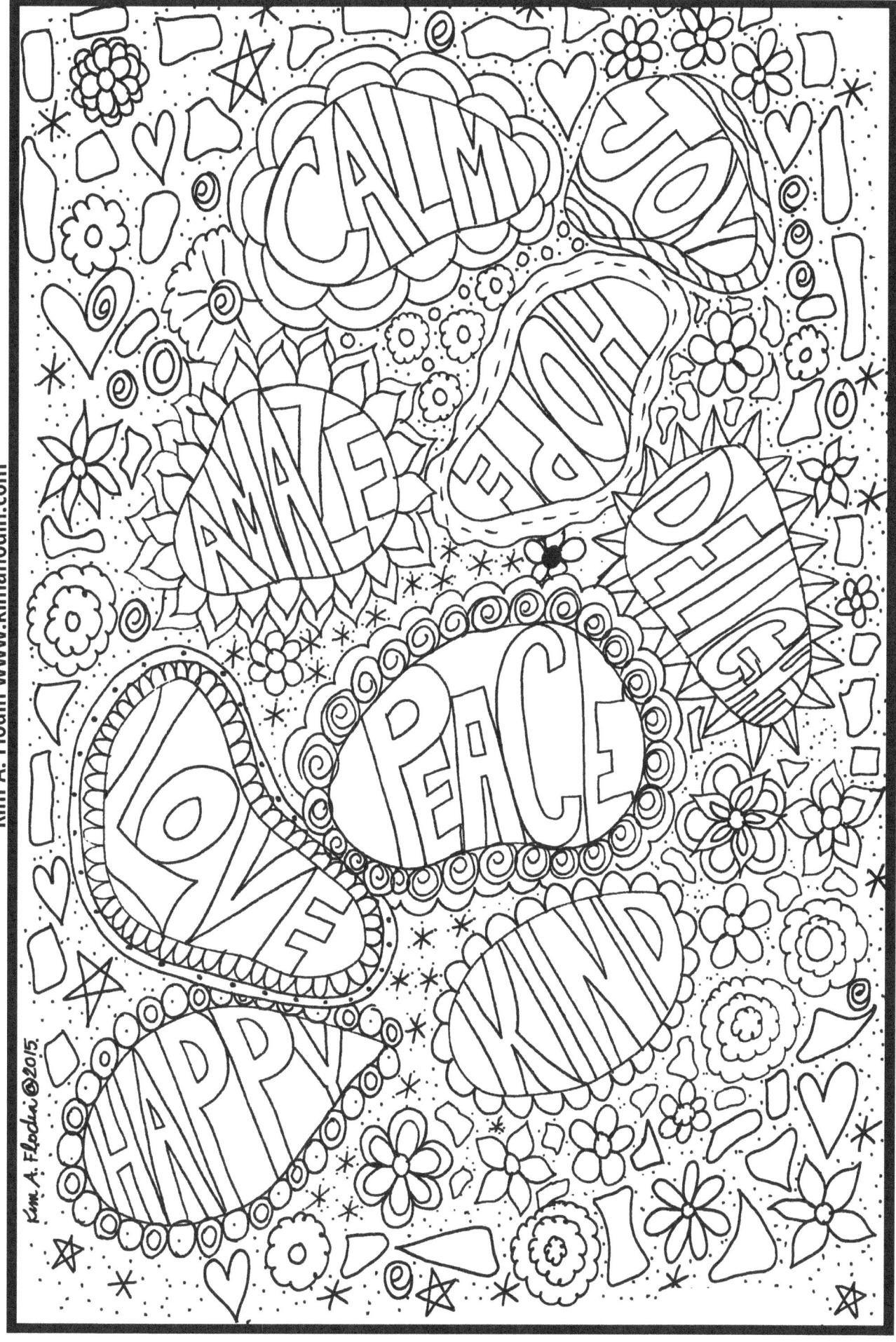

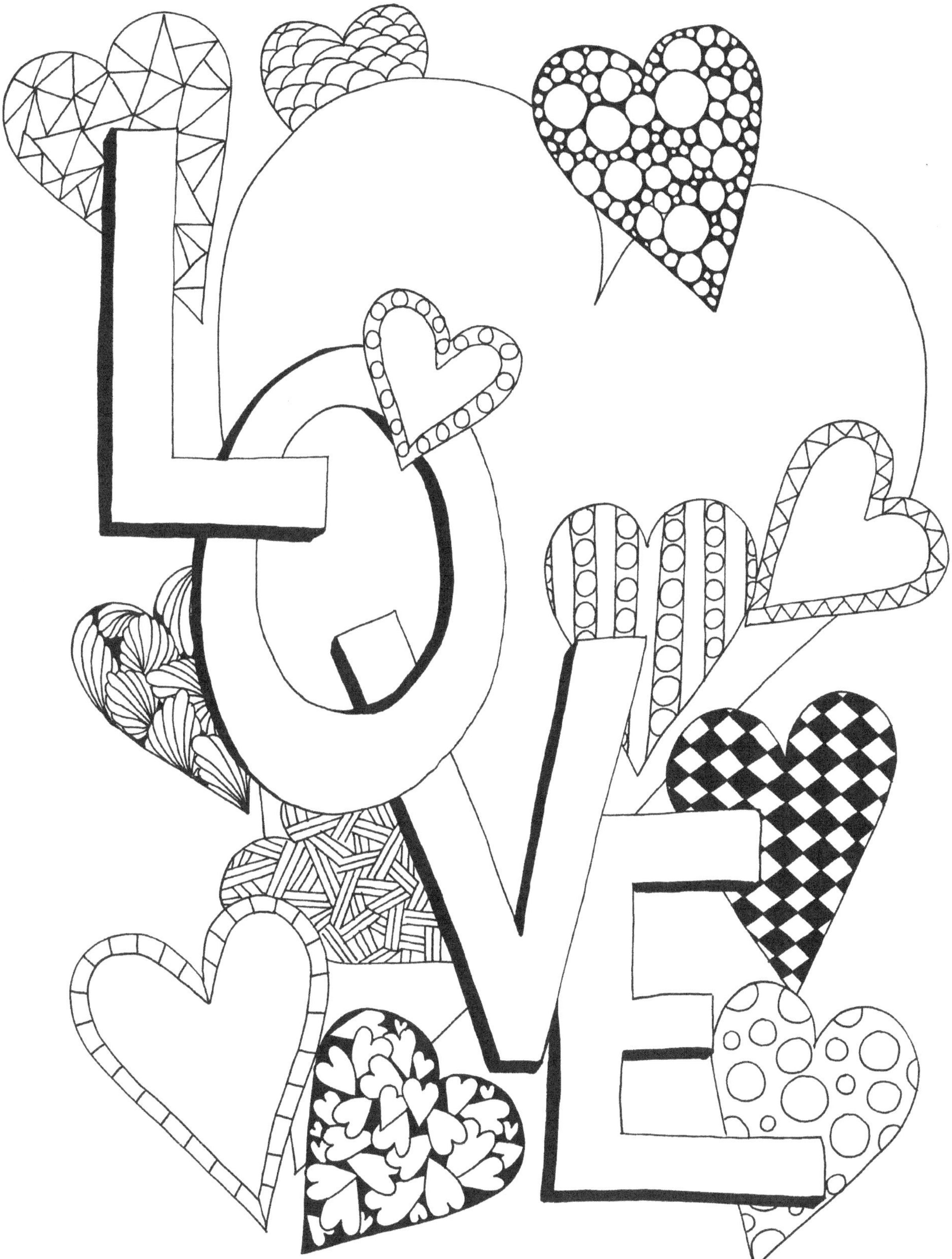

Lianne Lynch www.artunwound.com

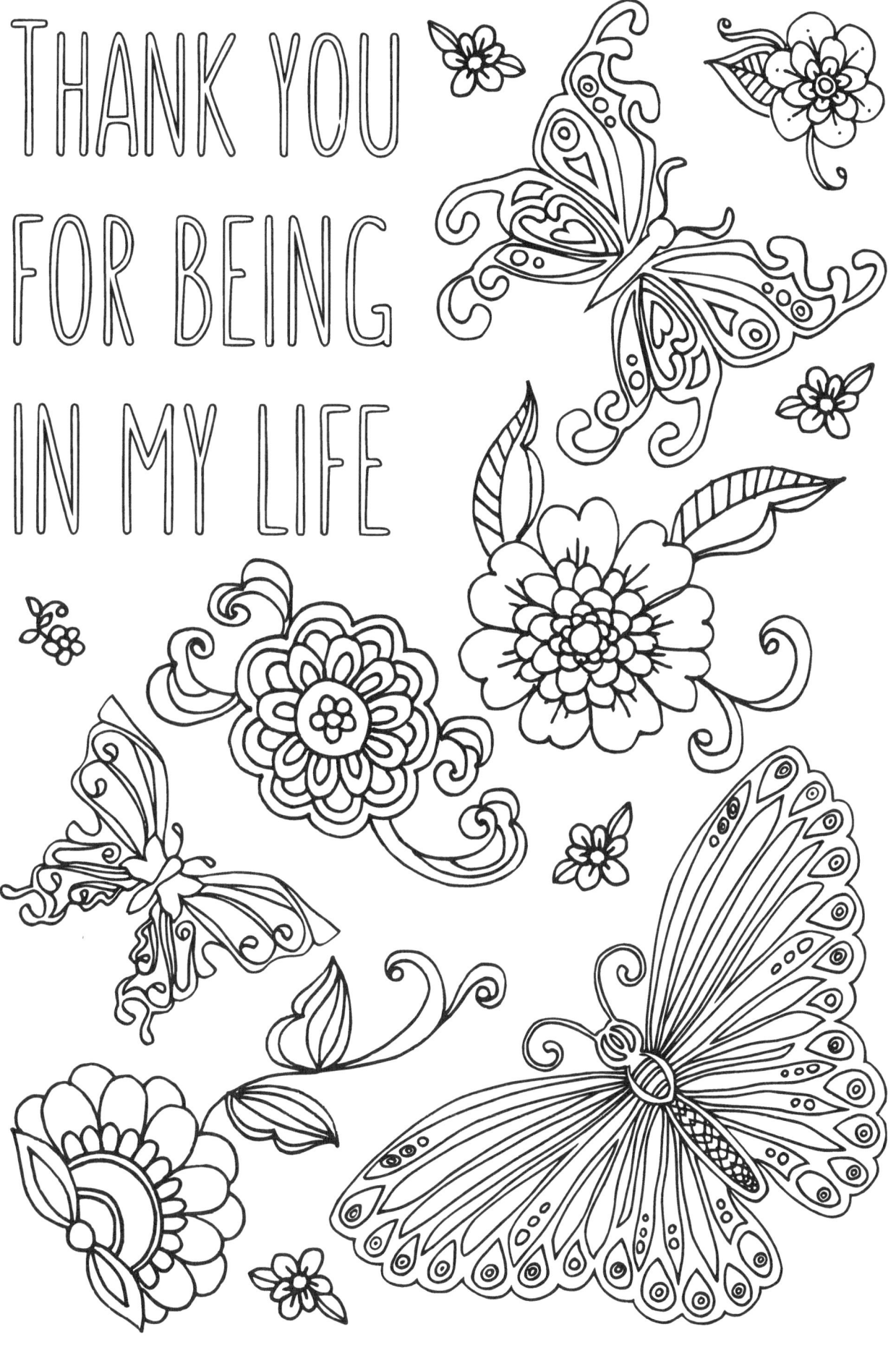

THANK YOU FOR BEING IN MY LIFE

Linda Franklin

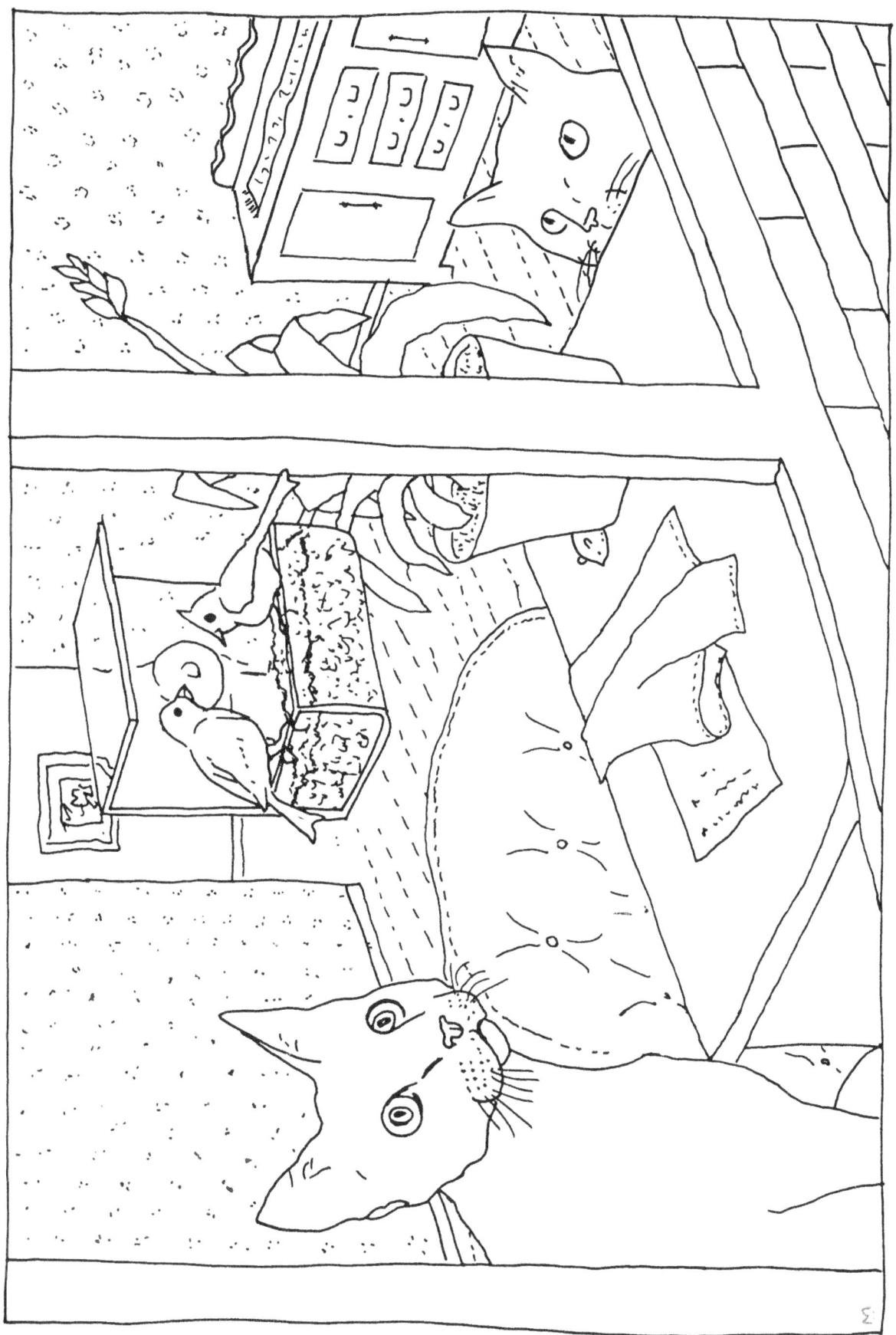

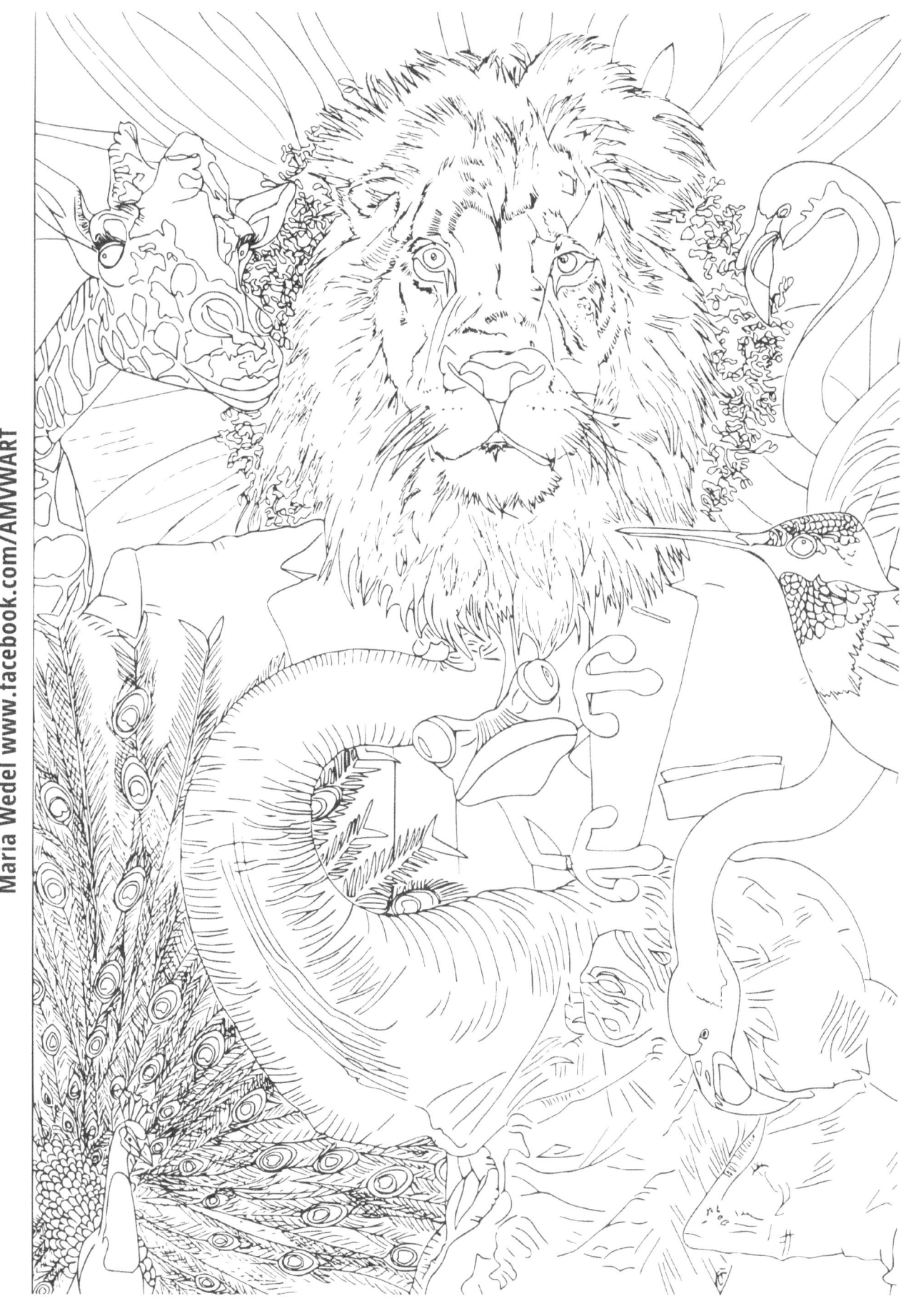

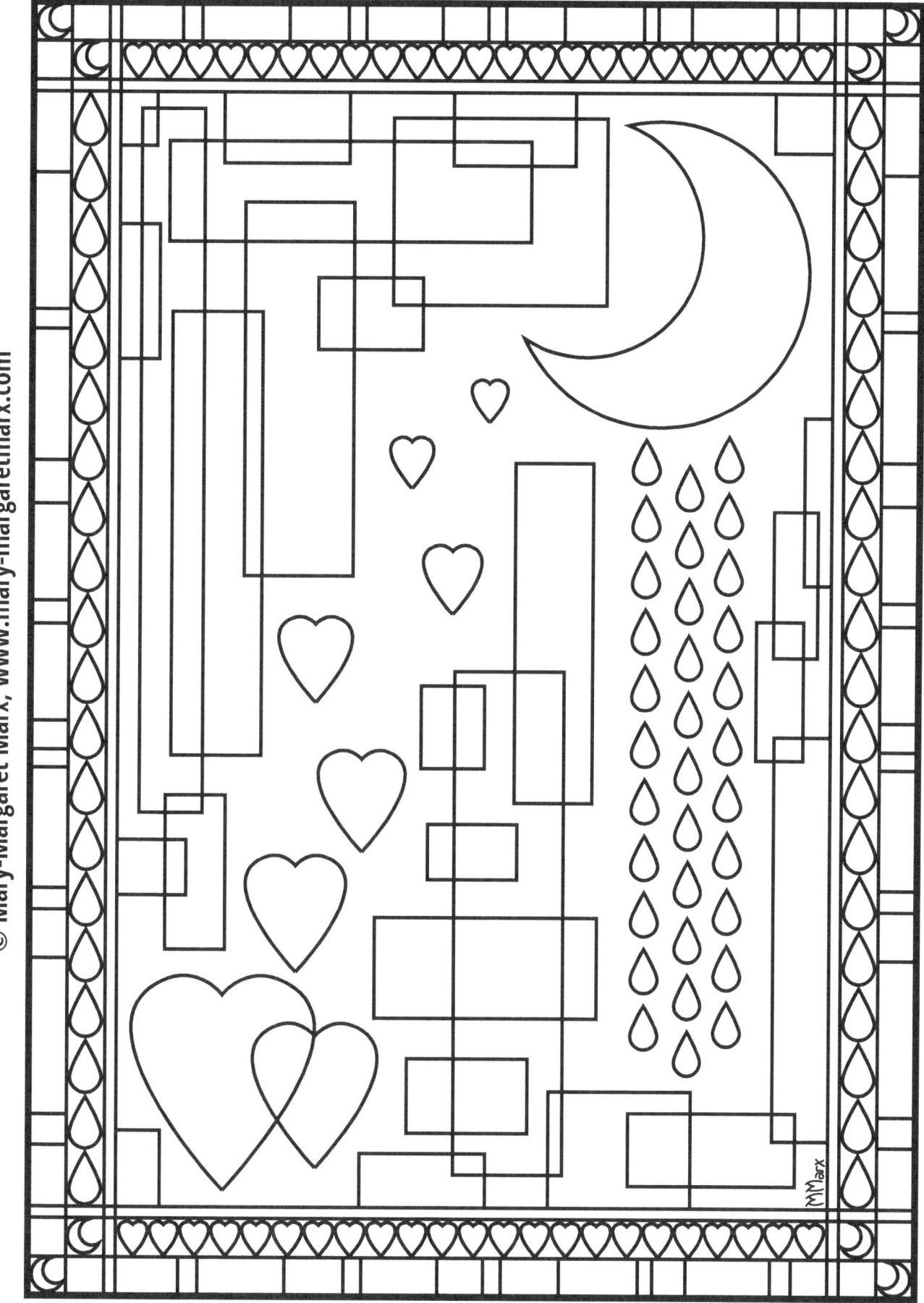

You are loved

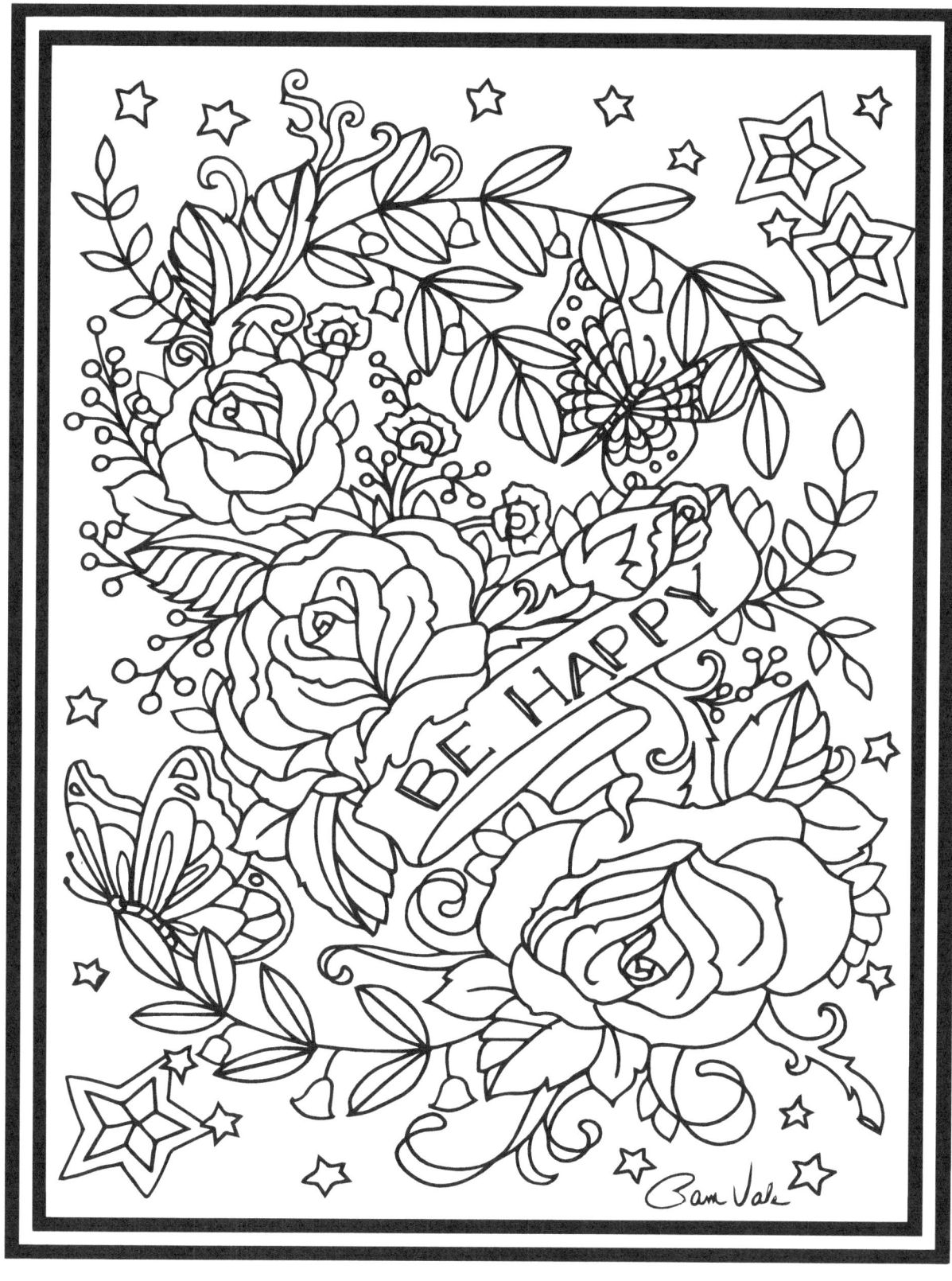

BE HAPPY

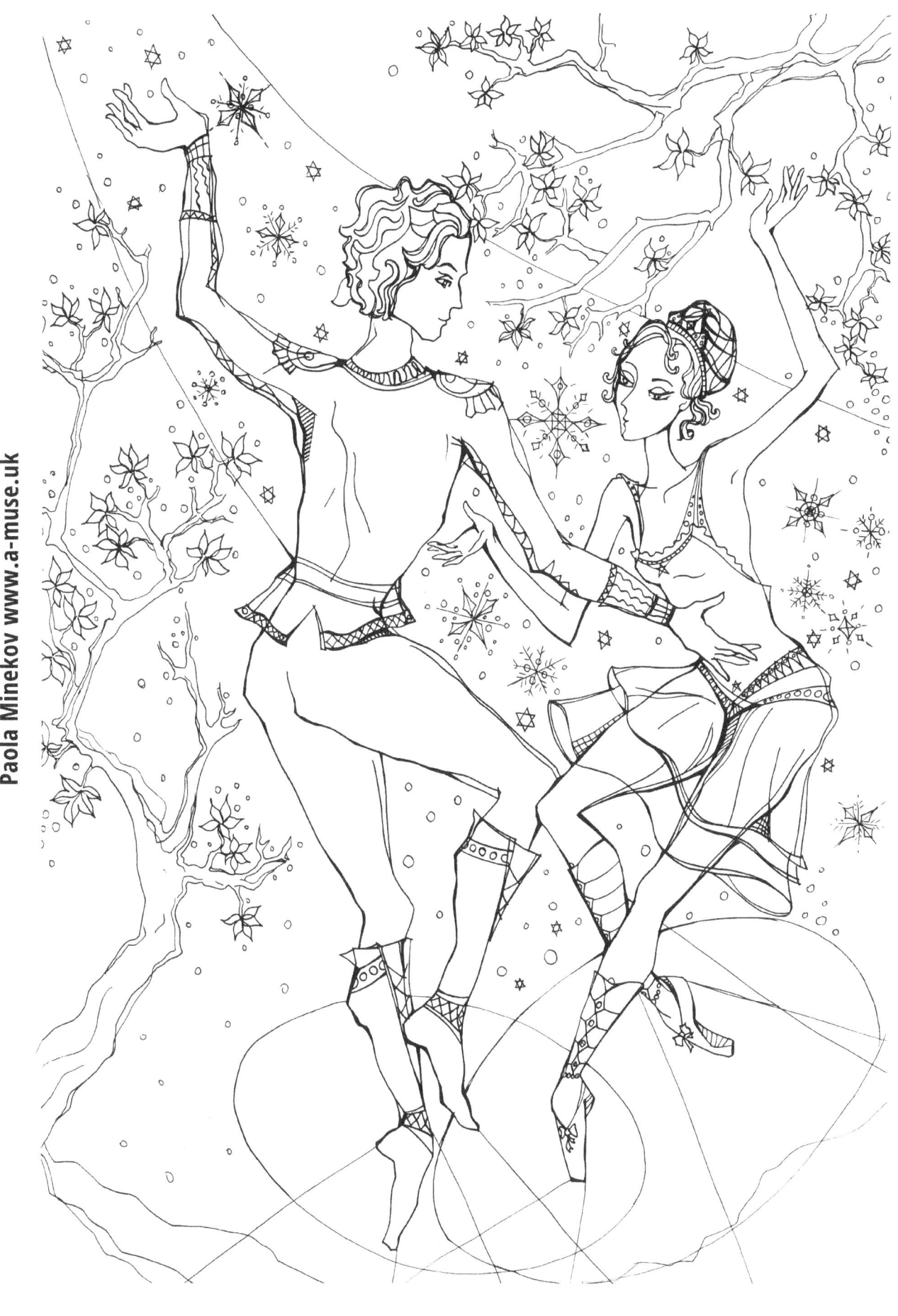

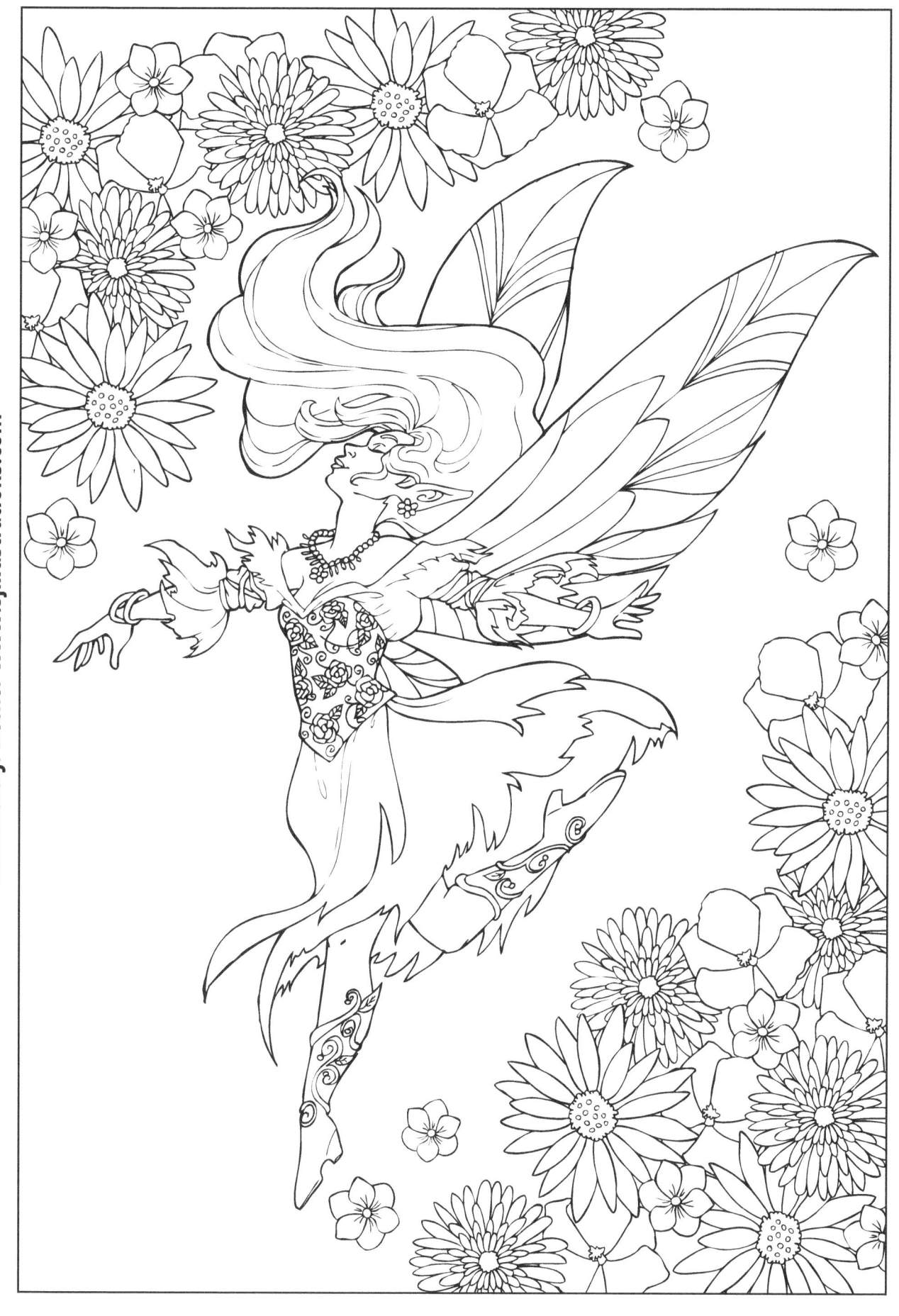

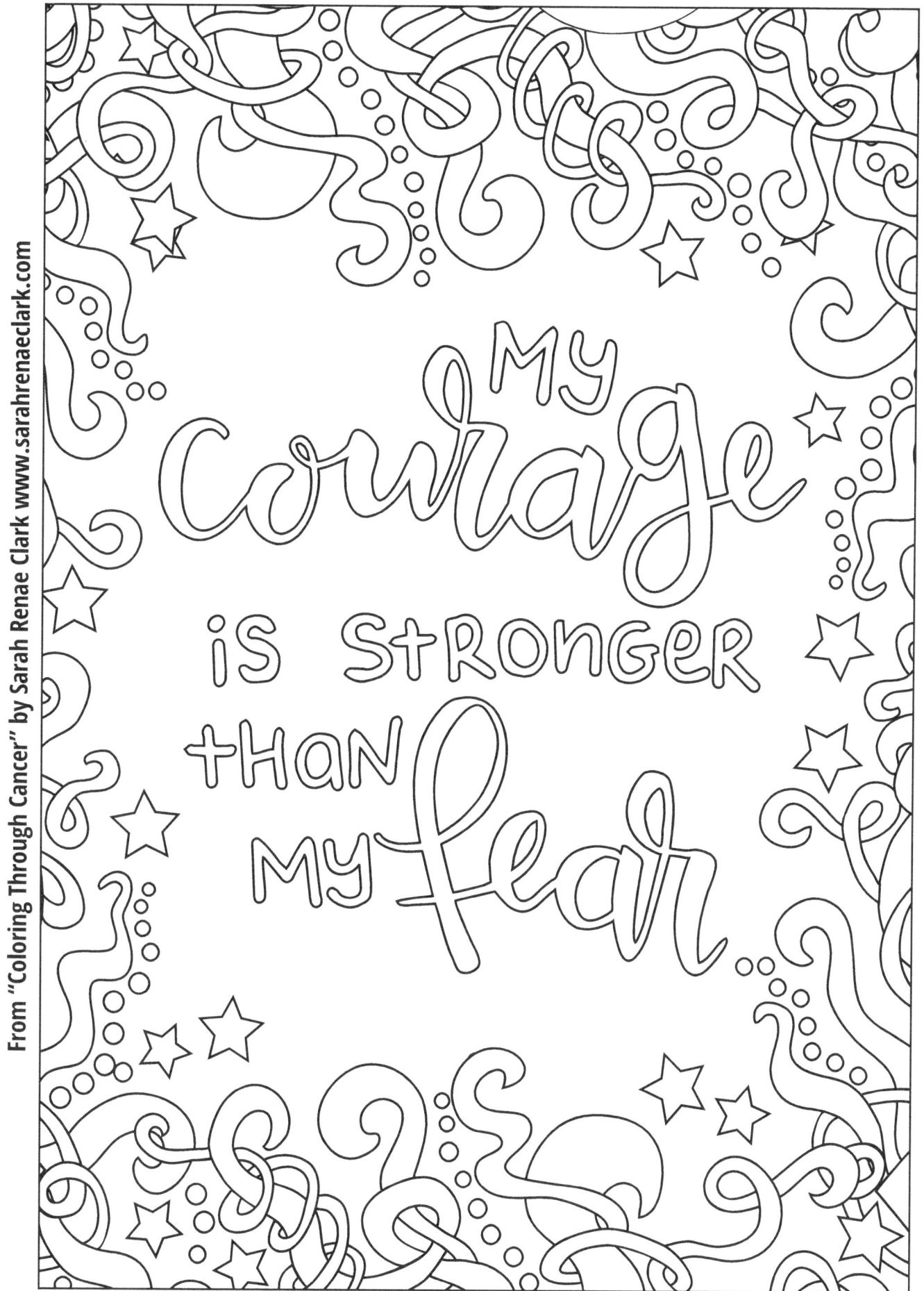

My courage is stronger than my fear

Believe
in You

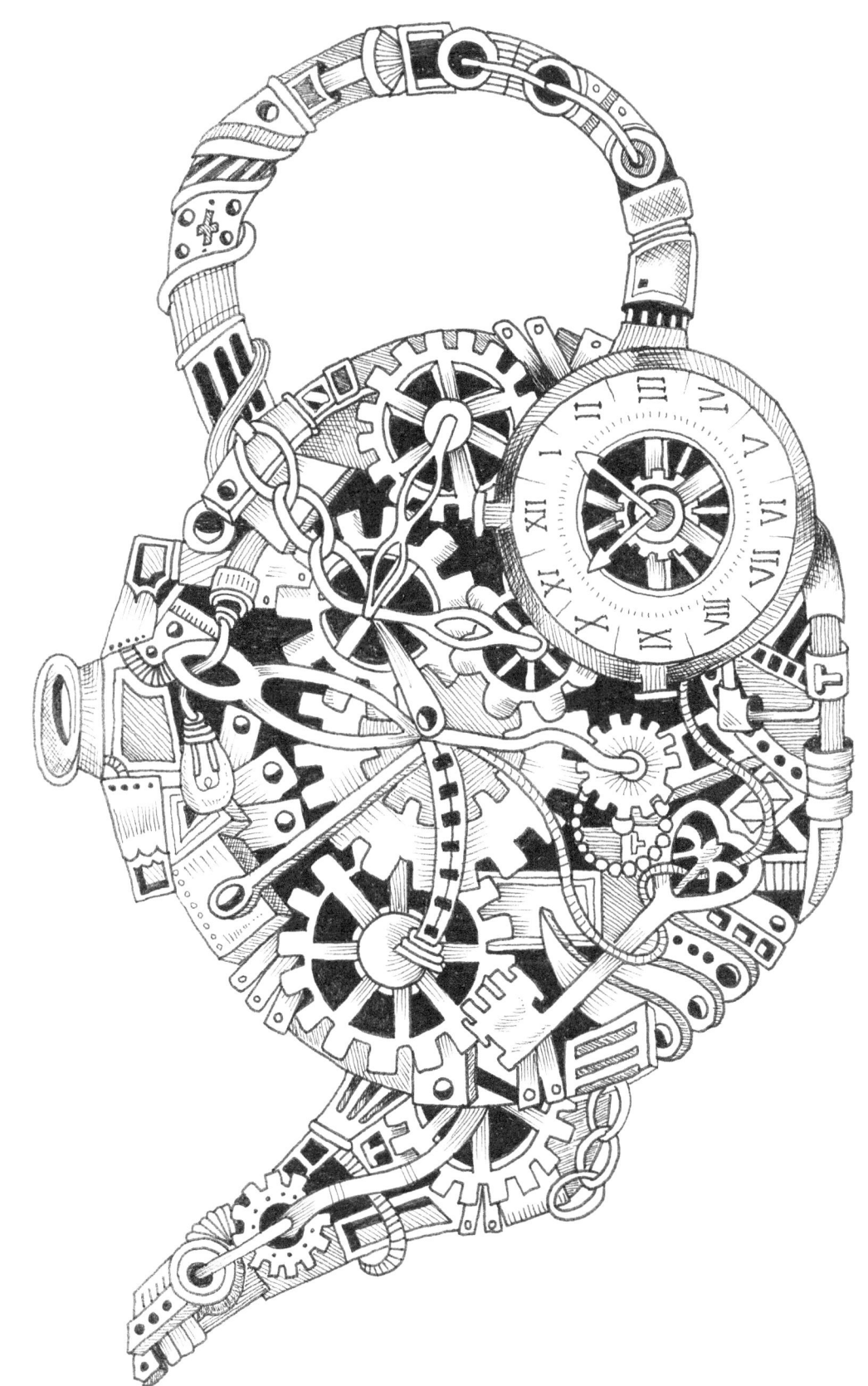

Make time for tea.

PERSEVERE

GIVE

HOPE

Sue Chastain - suziqcreations.com

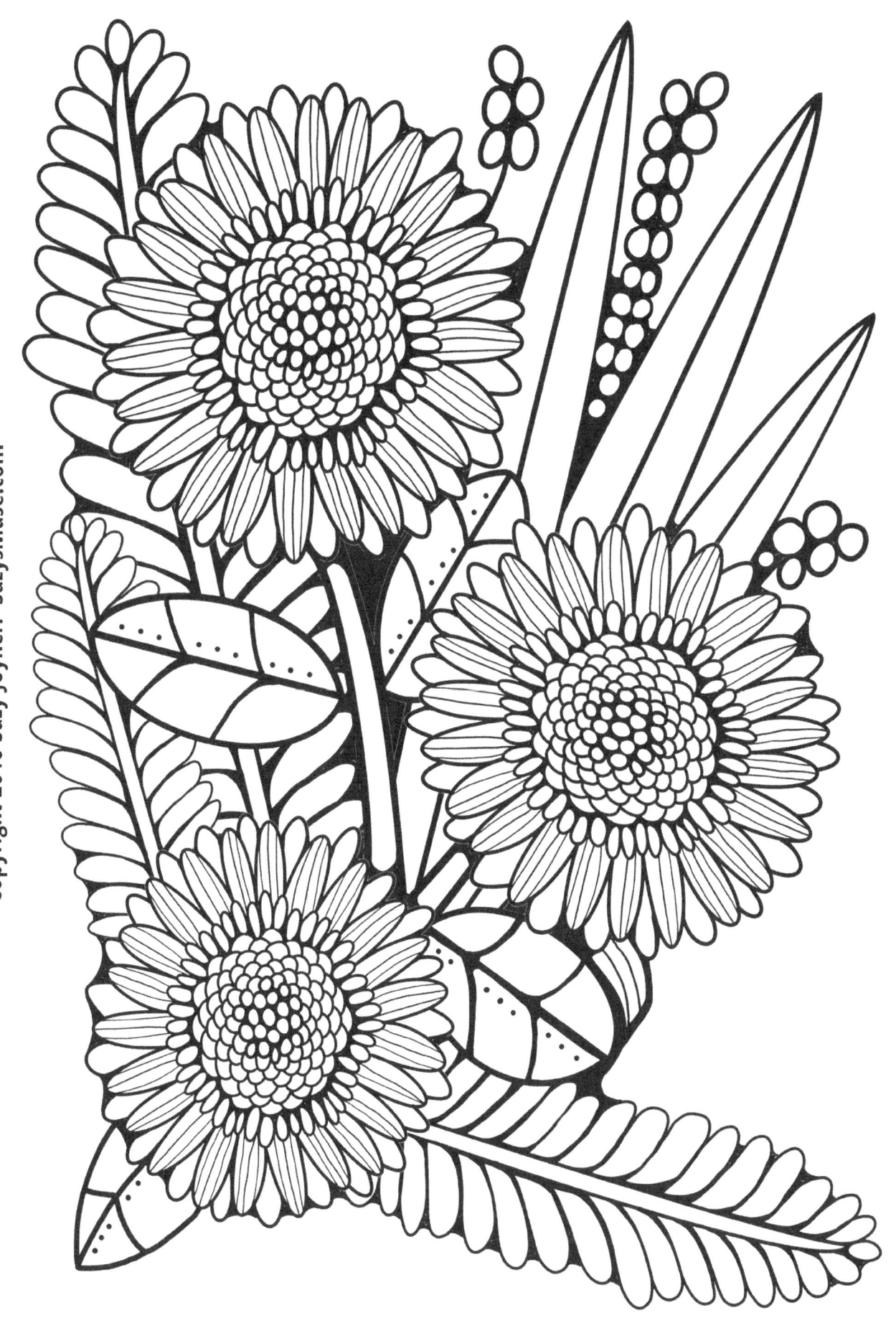

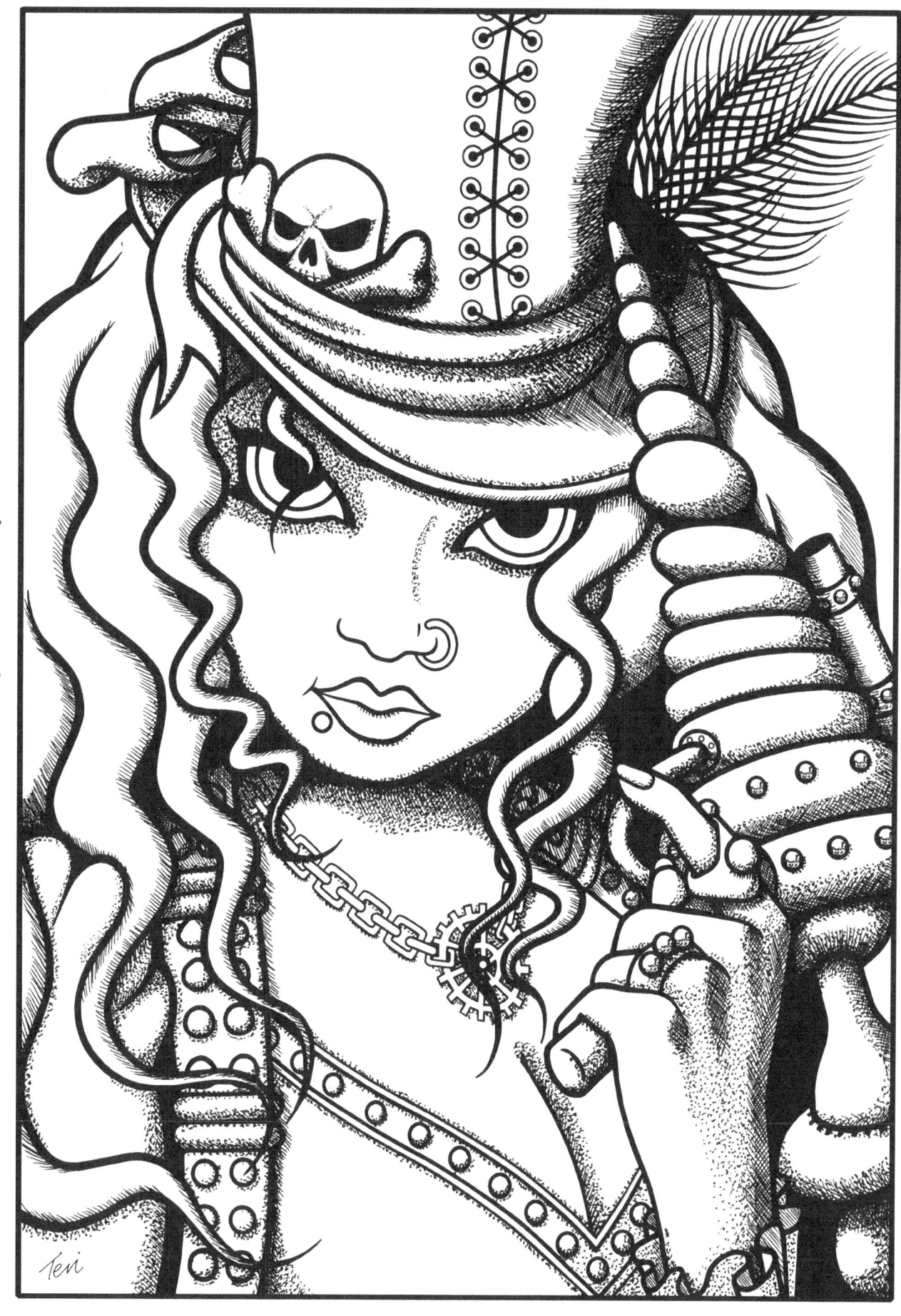

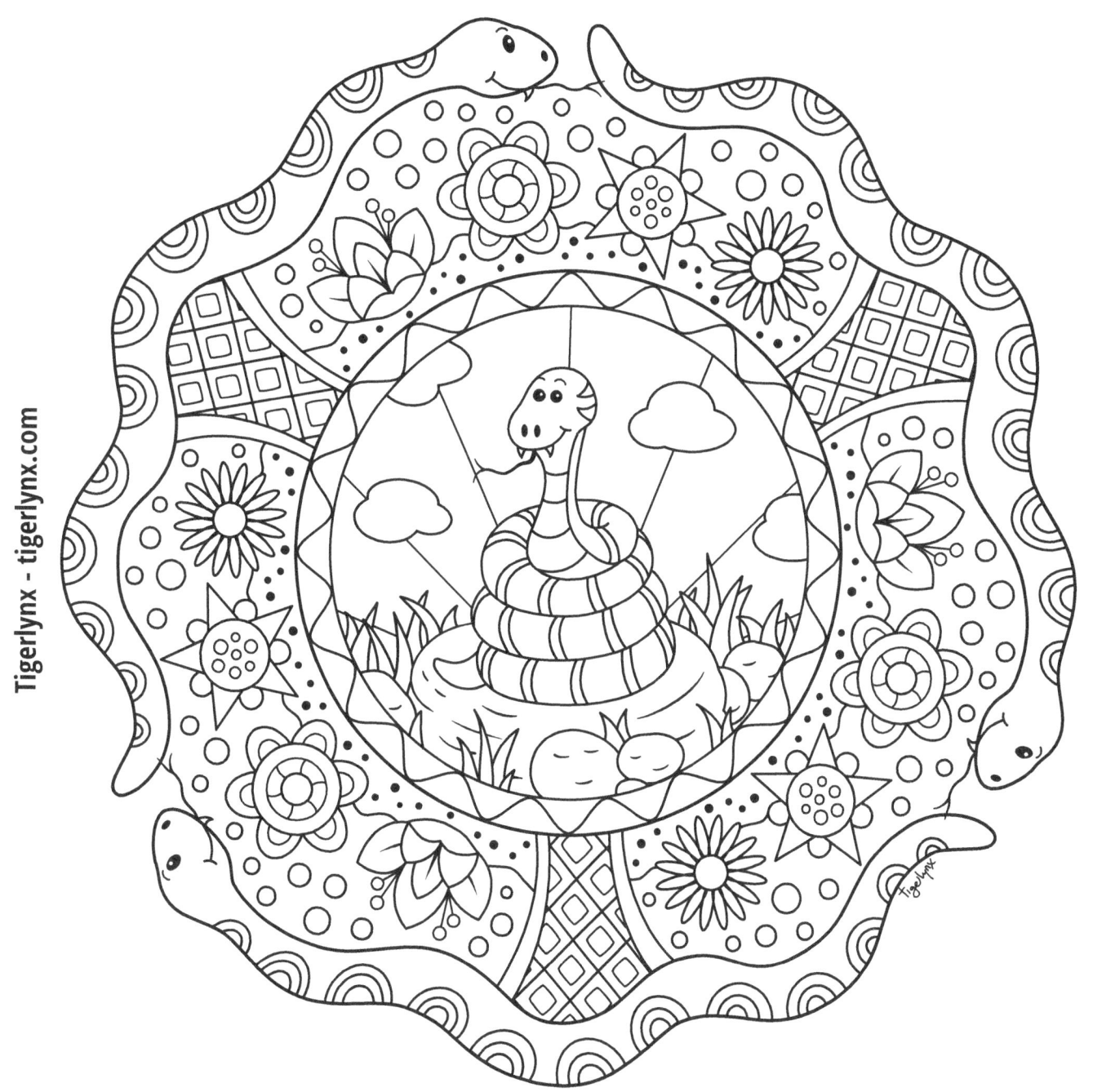

Bonus Images

These images were submitted by Daniel's very talented 10 year old daughter, Katie.

Katie has been regularly featured as an artist on Daniel's Facebook page:
facebook.com/savagescribbles

Katie Savage - facebook.com/savagescribbles

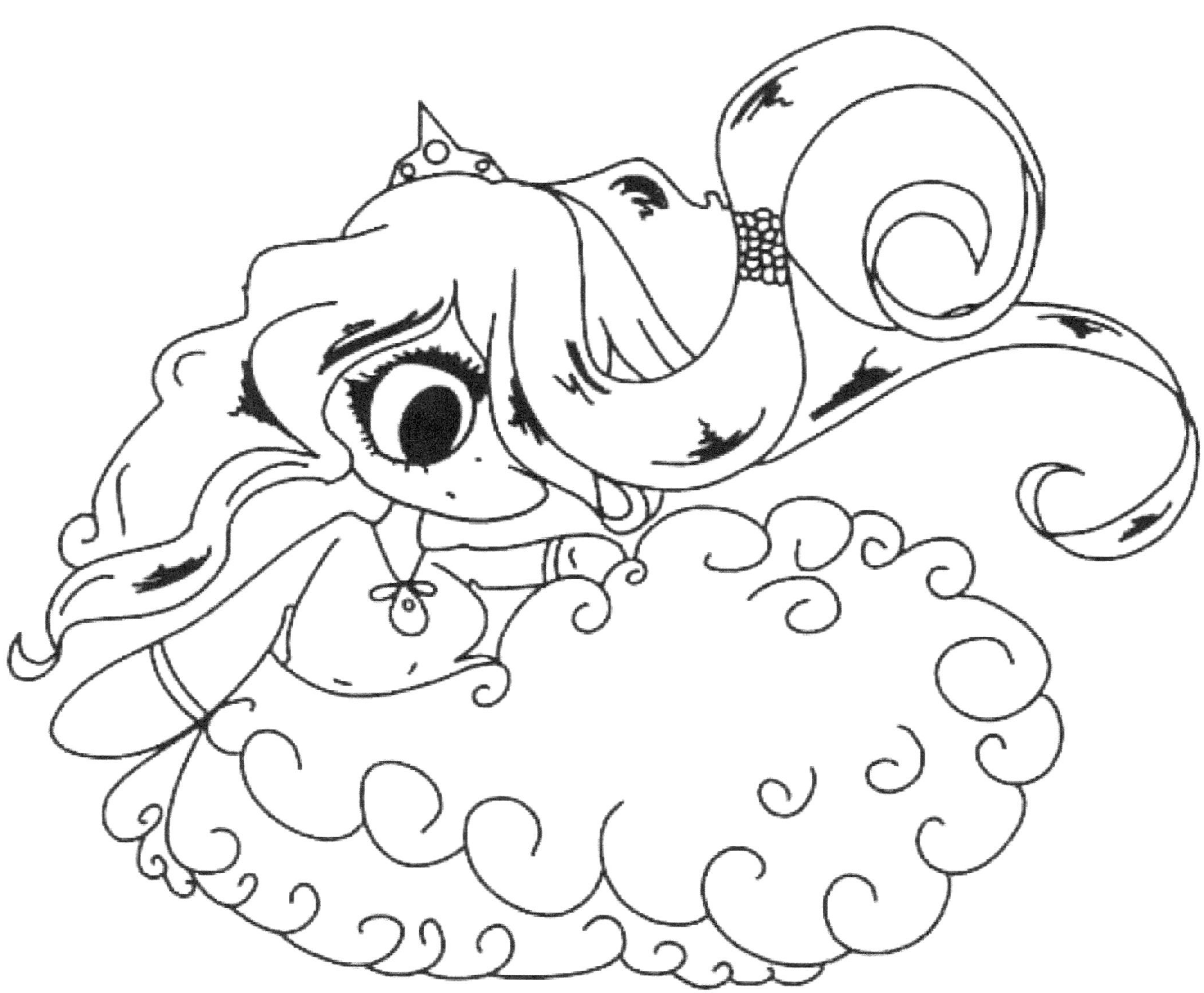

Katie Savage - facebook.com/savagescribbles

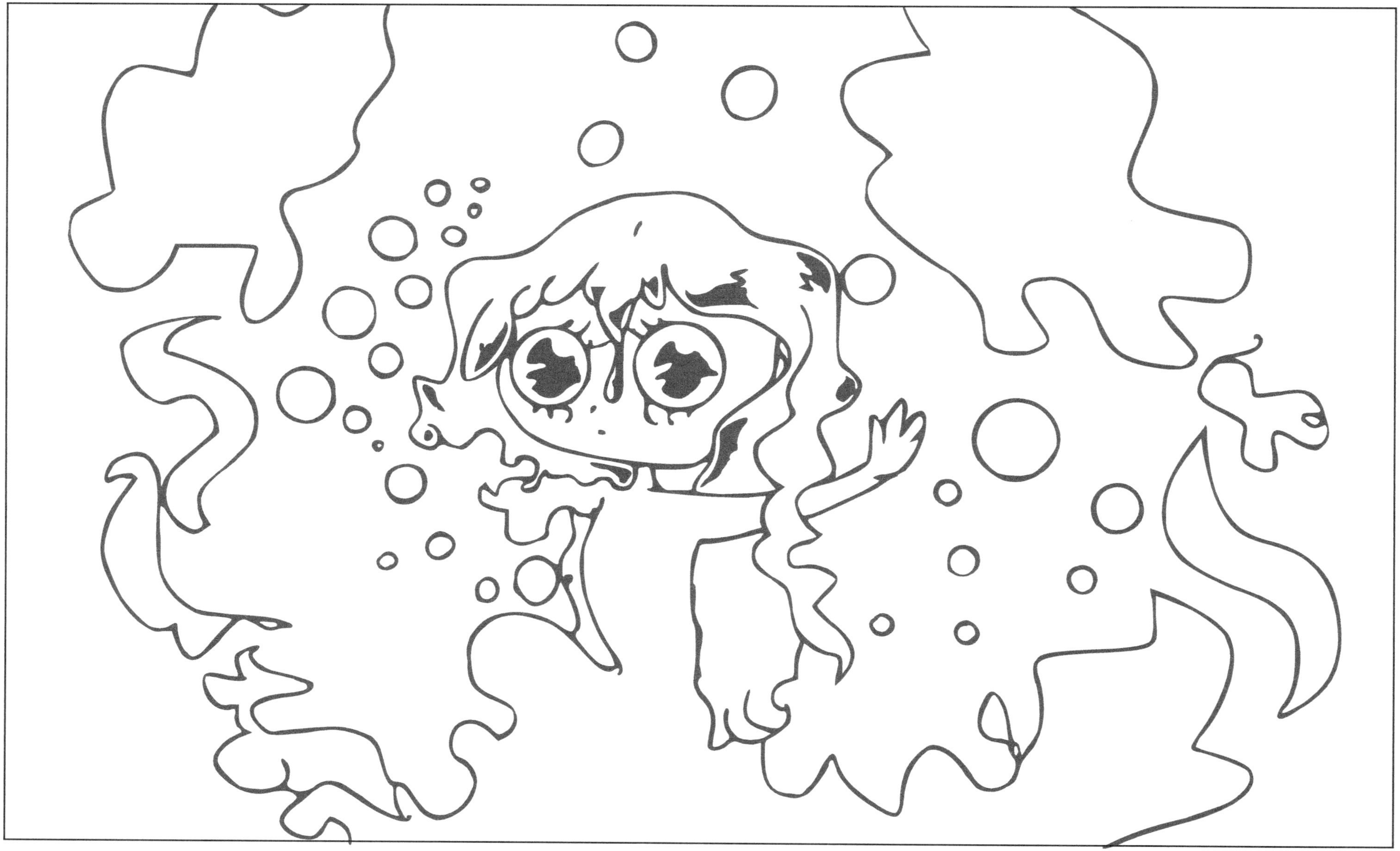

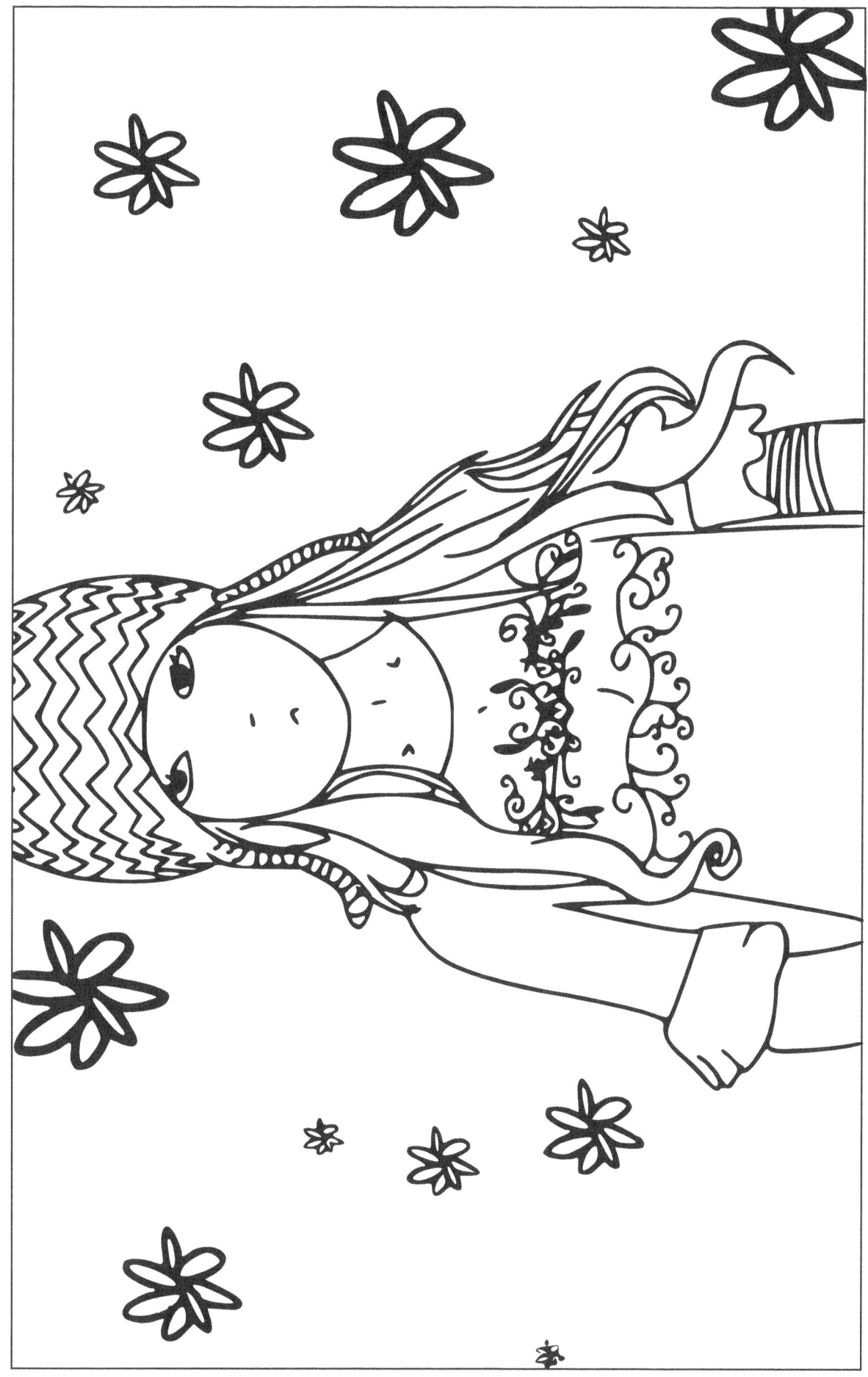

Katie Savage - facebook.com/savagescribbles

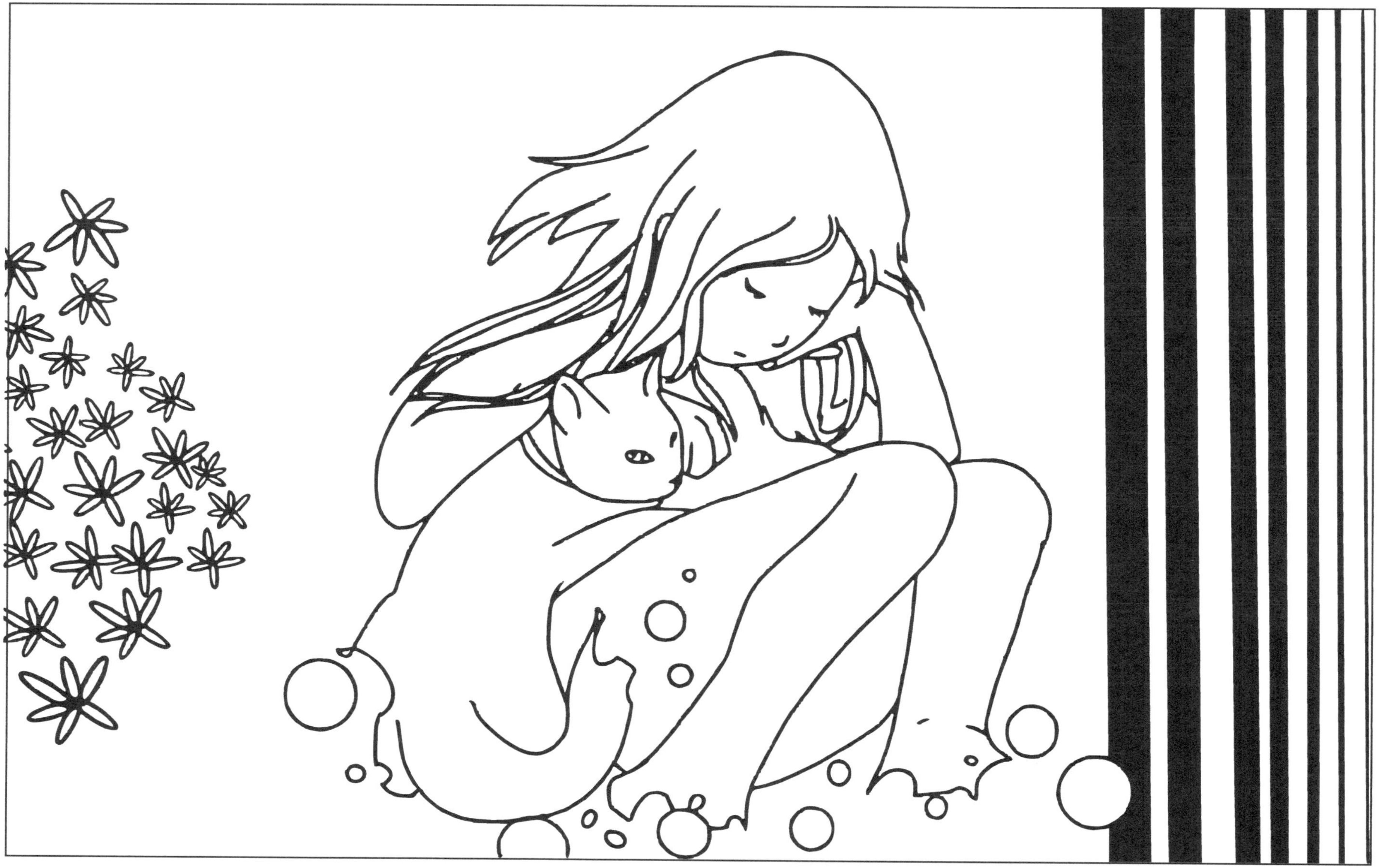

Use this page to test color combinations and as a blotter page

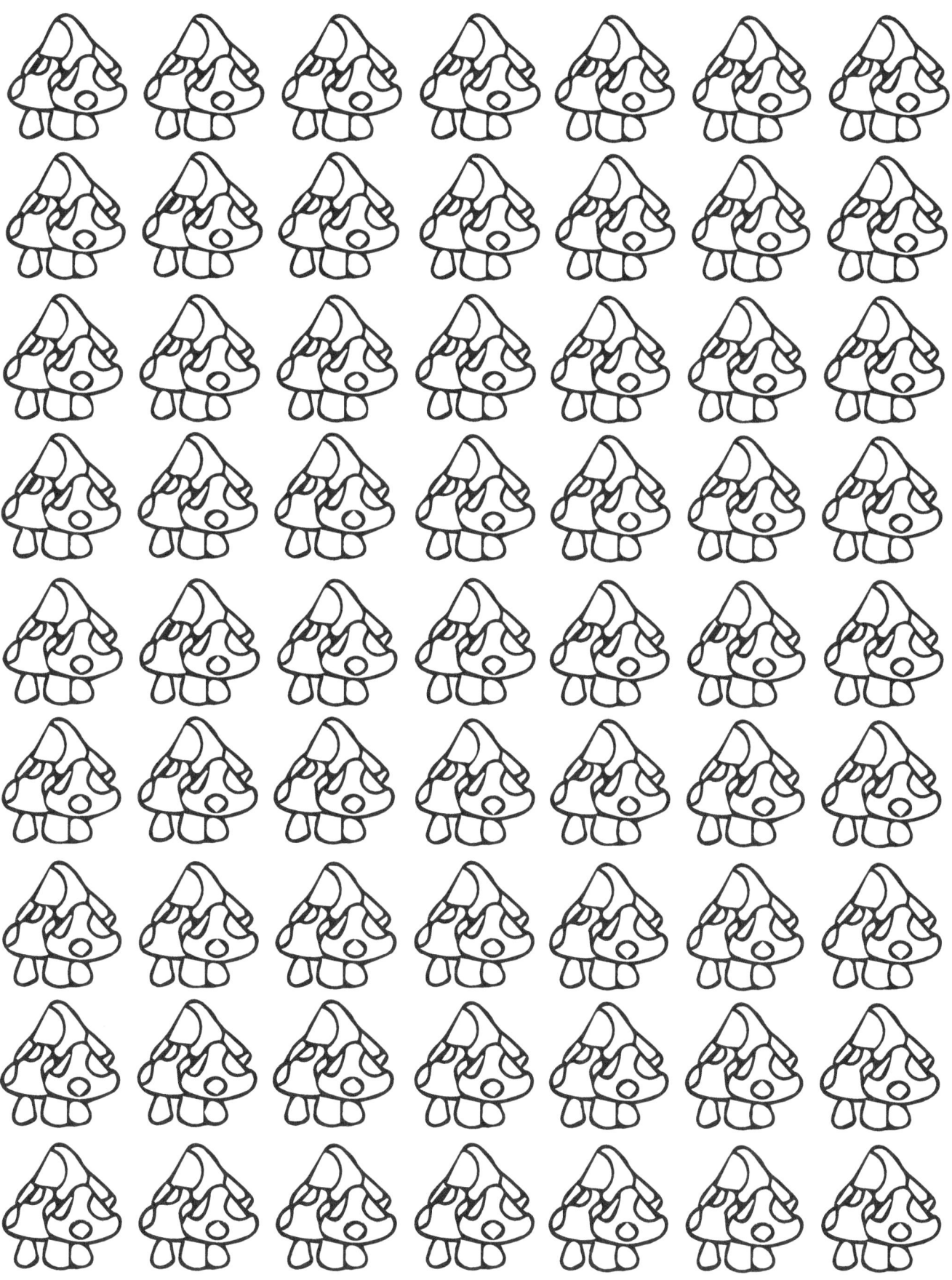

Use this page to test color combinations and as a blotter page

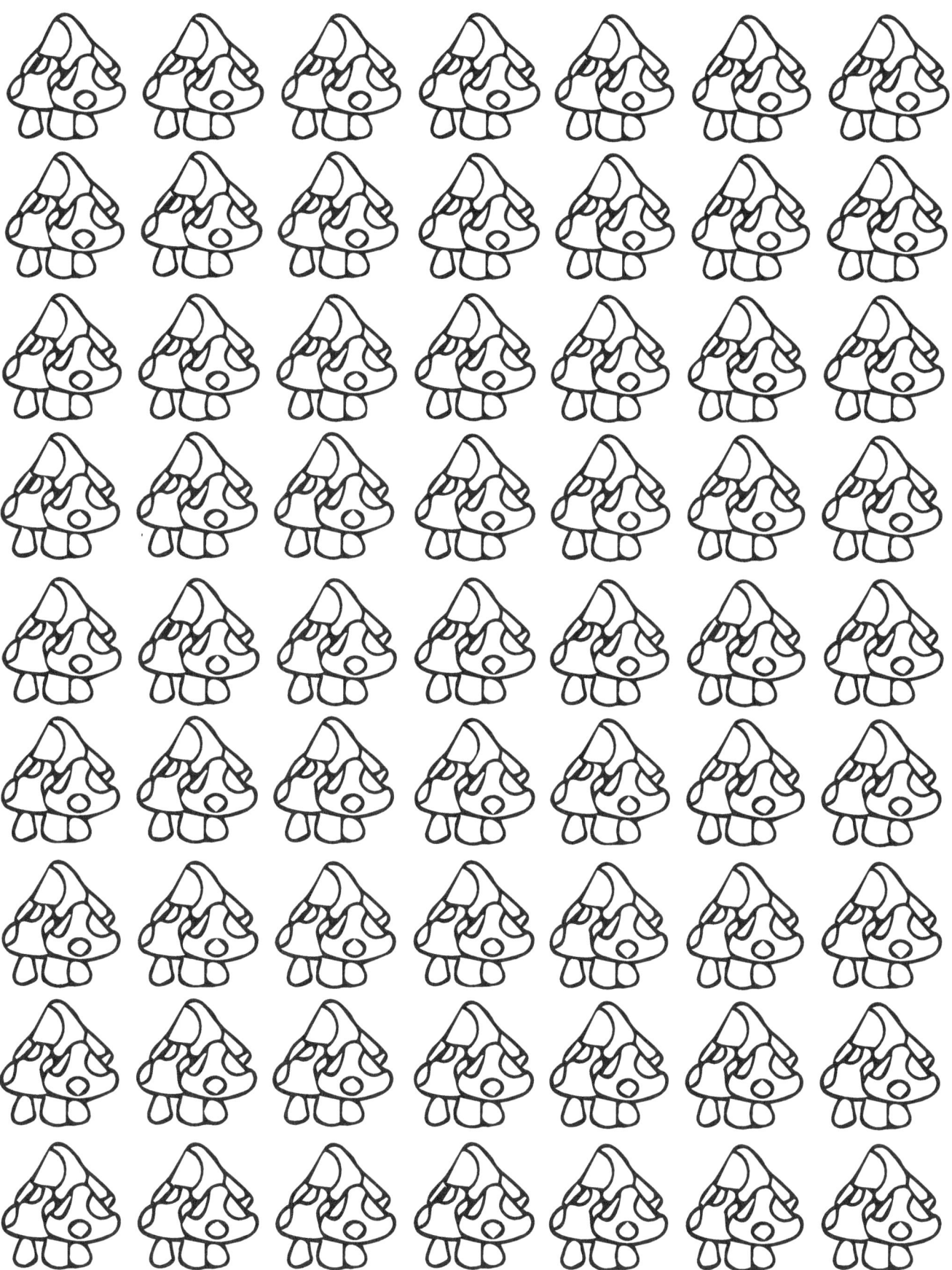

www.ingramcontent.com/pod-product-compliance
Lightning Source LLC
Chambersburg PA
CBHW081210180526
45170CB00006B/2292